RELIQUIAE

Landscape   Nature   Mythology

CORBEL STONE PRESS

Reliquiae

Volume 8 Number 1

ISSN 2398–7359

Edited by Autumn Richardson & Richard Skelton
Published by Corbel Stone Press

ISBN 978-1-9160951-2-0

*

*

*

*

*

*

*

*

207
End Matter
Notes & Bibliography

*

Each section is completed
by a selection of Dakota words

Reliquiae interleaves eco-logically aware writing from the past and present, rang-ing from the ethnological to the philosophical, the lyrical to the visionary. It is published biannually, in May and November.

RELIQUIAE

Kim Dorman
Kerala Journal (Excerpts)

Nightfall. Rats scamper
in the attic. The sinuous notes
of a nadhaswaram drift
from the nearby temple.
On the road, buses carry pilgrims
to Sabarimala. The winter air
is crisp. Numberless insects
chant to the stars.

.

atop a tall
wooden post
at the edge

of the paddy field,
a small blue
kingfisher

looks down,
watching
the water

.

My next door
neighbour tills his
small plot;
from the east
the smell of rain.

.

a light
blue shard
lies among
pebbles

overhead,
racket-tailed
drongos
spin, chase

.

The cool season has come;
work begins on houses, roads.

Piles of dead
leaves slowly burn.

As the long day fades, we
turn to the west.

Fruit bats fly toward the sun.

.

glimpse of
a small green
parakeet

for a moment
in the silk
cotton tree

.

Clouds in the east
like gilded rags.

Before sunrise,
silent birds cross the sky.

　　　.

This morning
we sat on the stone steps
in a cool breeze.

In the garden white
flowers (a kind of lily?)
attracted swarms

of tiny black bees.

　　　.

Rain drips on the
tin roof, frogs
& crickets chant.

The passing days
turn to years.

Lying awake in the
dark, I know the
taste of ash.

.

Evening is still as rain clouds
rise in the west. All the trees
are dark silhouettes: teak, jack,
coconut. The world is silent
but for the echoing cry
of a brain fever bird.

.

Far thunder recedes. Gray
light reflects from paddy fields.

What is the name of that flower,
dark as blood, dripping rain?

The clogged gutters overflow.
A silent crow flies past.

.

The rain has stopped,
darkness comes:
the day ends. Lamps
are lit in certain homes;
the fine scent of
hot coconut oil fills
the still air. At the end
of every wick, a white
immaterial pearl.
Luminous, steady...

(for Ella)

Steffi Lang
Residual

between one city and the other,
the salt path illumines the dark

      Scorpio coils over cinder hills,
lupine, larkspur, nettle-weed. hands
that under deserts, white
rootedness would keep

quartz formations, karst, and there
was memory in that clay

      every speaking was a waywardness,
shale and ash, silica, the thousand crushed songs
    of a ghost water — that even the hill-deer
    would be phosphorescent

and mouths would sip. that I gather myself
in such solitudes,   light is what I touch on
by attribute, no image,
but what the dusty field brings. *to find*
there, what language must I cross, what absence
must I bring

black leaf where birds leave their shadow
as fossil, death, how a sign
remembers this,
what stone falters —

Hildegard von Bingen
Lingua Ignota (Excerpts)

Among the works of the twelfth-century visionary abbess
of Rupertsberg, Hildegard von Bingen, is a secret language,
through which she encoded references to the spiritual,
human and natural worlds. Below is an excerpt of fifty of
her coinages — those for trees and shrubs.

Lamischiz	*Abies*	fir
Pazimbu	*Mespilus*	medlar [1]
Schalmindibuz	*Amigdalus*	almond [2]
Bauschuz	*Acer*	maple
Hamischa	*Alnus*	alder
Laizscia	*Tilia*	lime
Scoibuz	*Buxus*	box
Gramzibuz	*Castanea*	chestnut
Scoica	*Carpenus*	hornbeam [3]
Bumbirich	*Corilus*	hazel [4]
Zaimzabuz	*Cydonia*	quince [5]

Gruzimbuz	*Cerasus*	cherry [6]
Culmendiabuz	*Cornus*	dogwood
Guskaibuz	*Esculus*	h. chestnut [7]
Gigunzibuz	*Ficus*	fig
Bizarmol	*Fraxinus*	ash
Zamzila	*Fagus*	beech
Scoimchia	*Picea*	spruce
Scongilbuz	*Fusarius*	spindle [8]
Clamizibuz	*Laurus*	laurel
Gonizla	*Studa*	?
Zaschibuz	*Lentiscus*	pistachio [9]
Schamihilbuz	*Iuniperus*	juniper [10]
Pomziaz	*Malus*	apple
Mizamabuz	*Morus*	mulberry
Burschiabuz	*Murica*	myrtle [11]
Laschiabuz	*Ornus*	ash
Golinzia	*Platanus*	plane
Sparinichibuz	*Persicus*	peach [12]
Zirumzibuz	*Pirus*	pear
Burzimibuz	*Prinus*	plum [13]
Gimeldia	*Pinus*	pine
Noinz	*Paliurus*	buckthorn
Lamschiz	*Riscus*	*broom* [14]
Scinzibuz	*Sauina*	*savin* [15]
Kisanzibuz	*Chinus*	?
Ornalzibuz	*Sanguinarius*	*dog's berry* [16]
Vischobuz	*Taxus*	yew
Gulizbaz	*Uibex*	*birch* [17]
Scoiaz	*Uimina*	*osier* [18]
Wagiziaz	*Salix*	willow
Scuanibuz	*Mirtus*	myrtle [19]
Schirobuz	*Acer*	*sycamore* [20]
Orschibuz	*Quercus*	oak
Muzimibuz	*Nucus*	?

Gisgiaz	*Tribulus*	thistle
Zizanz	*Dumi*	*thorn* [21]
Izziros	*Uepres*	?
Gluuiz	*Arundo*	*cane* [22]
Ausiz	*Cicuta*	w. hemlock

Editors' Notes:

The first column lists von Bingen's words, the second lists Latin glosses provided by Elias Steinmeyer and Eduard Sievers (1895). We have provided the English versions in the third column — italics indicating a provisional entry.

1   Translated as 'nespelbŏm/nesbilbŏm' by Steinmeyer and Sievers, which appear to be German folknames for *Mespilus germanica*, the medlar tree.

2   *Amigdalus=Amygdalus?*

3   *Carpenus=Carpinus?*

4   *Corilus=Corylus?*

5   Translated as 'cutinbŏm', which appears to be a German folkname for the quince tree.

6   Now *Prunus*.

7   *Esculus=Aesculus?*

8   *Fusarius* cannot be identified with any plant genera. *Fusaria*, however, is identified with the German folkname 'spinnilboum' by Hildebrant and Ridder (1995), which equates with *Euonymus*, or spindle.

9   *Lentiscus* now *Pistacia*.

10 *Iuniperus* now *Juniperus*.

11 *Murica=Myrica?*

12 *Persicus=Prunus persica?*

13 Hildebrant and Ridder identify Prinus with 'phlumboum', which, in turn, Graff (1837) associates with 'pflaumenbaum', which is the subgenera *Prunus Prunus*, or plum.

14 Possibly *Ruscus aculeatus*, or butcher's broom.

15 Possibly *Juniperus sabina*, the savin juniper.

16 Possibly *Cornus sanguinea*, dog's berry, or common dogwood. See Gerard (1597).

17 Possibly *Uibex=Vibex*, which Hildebrant and Ridder equate with 'birka', i.e. *Betula*, or birch.

18 Possibly *Salix viminalis*, common osier.

19 *Mirtus=Myrtus?*

20 Translated as 'ahornenbŏm', 'maple tree', but see Bauschuz, *Acer*. Sycamore, as as species of *Acer*, is therefore suggested.

21 Hildebrant and Ridder identify *Dumi* with 'dorn', thorn.

22 Possibly *Arundo donax*, giant cane.

Jane Lovell
Landmarks

I will tell you stories of the sea and trace its currents on your palm, the shape of a tern's wing, the curve of a whale's back, the flit and shift of fish fleeing seal-song. Feel it and remember you are smaller than a pebble in the sea's roar.

Sunlight falls in slabs on bloodied floes;
tusks, skins, flesh stacked,
we head for shore.

Look to the winds: the slant of frozen grass, melt-water brimming at the far call of a lake, black straggles of wind-rushed trees, nubs of foliage sheltering in their lee. Snow-rise can fix you. *Kaioqlaq* and *tumarinyiq* will betray the paths of the dead; track them, north, north east.

Winds from the south thin
the lake's edge; glimpse of blue depths,
eyes of a young seal.

Take care with the stars that never move, and the thinning spring sky, its mists. Three stars running will guide you. *Sakiatsiat* and *Tukturjuit*, and the seal-hunter who rose from death to burn in the southern sky, he that steers the night's shadows.

Green light, east to west;
blown snow catches lunar drift.
Soft we step, unsure.

A water sky betrays the sea, its clouds black with kelp and krill. Hypnotised by the frantic seethe of life, the sea laps its dirty tongue and spits salt. Above it hang dreams of basking walrus, boats, lands beyond the curve.

Suspended in light
conjured by treacherous seas,
I dream I am bird.

R.P. Masani
Some Water Folklore

The priestess of Gulval Well in Fosses Moor was an old woman who instructed the devotees in their ceremonial observances. They had to kneel down and lean over the well so as to see their faces in the water and repeat after their instructor a rhyming incantation, after which, the reply of the spirit of the well was interpreted by the bubbling of the water or its quiescence.

*

Near the well of St. Aelian, not far from Betteas Abergeley in Denbighshire, resided a woman who officiated as a kind of priestess. Any one who wished to inflict a curse upon an enemy resorted to this priestess, and for a trifling sum she registered in a book kept for the purpose the name of the person on whom the curse was intended to fall. A pin was then dropped into the well in the name of the victim and the curse was complete.

*

At the foot of Carn Brea Hill is a little well dedicated to St. Eunius. To be baptised in the water drawn from this is a sure safeguard against death by hanging.

*

It is impossible to remove the stones of the well of St.Cleer, which is situated near Liskeard. True, they may be carted away at daytime, but they all return at night and deposit themselves in heaps on the site from which they were taken. Similar stories are related of the marvellous powers of the basin which catches the water as it issues from the spring at St. Nun's Well, Pelynt, near Looe, and of the Bisland Holy Well, the ground surrounding which can never be broken for tillage on penalty of disaster to the family of the person attempting to do so.

*

There is in Mirzapur a famous water-hole, known as Barewa. A herdsman was once grazing his buffaloes near the place, when the waters rose in fury and carried him off with his cattle. The drowned buffaloes have now taken the form of a dangerous demon known as *Bhainsasura*, or the buffalo-demon, and he lives there in company with the Naga and the Nagan and none dare fish there until he has propitiated these demons with the offerings of a fowl, eggs and goat.

*

In the island of Chios is a bridge called the Maid's Bridge, which is popularly believed to be haunted by a water-spirit. Early one morning a man was crossing the bridge on his way from the village of Daphnona to the capital city, when he met a tall young woman dressed in white. She took him by the hand and made him dance with her. He was foolish enough to speak and was immediately struck dumb. He recovered, however, some days after, thanks to the prayers and exorcisms of a priest.

*

The worst of all ill-omened streams in India is the dread Vaitaranî, the river of death, which is localised in Orissa and which pours its stream of ordure and blood on the confines of the realm of Yama.

*

Plato says there are three kinds of sirens – the celestial,
the generative and the cathartic. The first are under the
government of Jupiter, the second under the government of
Neptune, and the third under the government of Pluto. When
the soul is in heaven, the sirens seek, by harmonic motion,
to unite it to the divine life of the celestial host; and when in
Hades, to conform them to the infernal regimen, but on earth
they produce generation, of which the sea is emblematic.

*

Many of the continental water deities must needs have human
sacrifices, just as the African river spirit Prah, who must have
every year in October two human sacrifices, one male and one
female. Thus in England the River Tees, the Skerne, and the
Ribble have each a sprite, who, in popular belief, demands
human victims. The Ribble's sprite is known by the name of
Peg O' Nell, and a spring in the grounds of Waddow bears her
name and is graced by a stone image, now headless, which,
according to Sir Laurence Gomme, is said to represent her.

*

Where the beautiful Neckar flows under the ruins of
Heidleberg Castle, the spirit of the river seeks to drown
three persons, one on Midsummer Eve, one on Midsummer
Day, and one on the day after. On these nights if you hear
a shriek, as of a drowning man or woman from the water,
beware of running to the rescue; for it is only the water-fairy
shrieking to lure you to your doom.

C.S. Mills
Apian heathen hof

Just past Beltane, nearing sunset in the marsh behind the
ruins, where the line of maples along the bluff casts long lan-
cet shadows in the low spring sun, the choir warms its voice.

> *Come antigone: you echo-maker,*
> *join the polyphony*
> *Come rising crucible: dayspring,*
> *our torpor has been long*
> *Come sweet spring, holy days of nectar*
> *Come ponderous priestess*

Beneath the boughs of the apple in resplendent soft pink
bloom, the apse. Bumblebees throw themselves from blos-
som to blossom, thrashing in their revelry, covered in yellow
pollen, seeking nectar; here they receive the body and the
blood. Phasing staccato swells arrive from the marsh.

> *O Echo, O Portent,*
> *mingle at the base*
> *Teach us the ritual: memory of yet-to-be,*
> *bring us fruit*
> *O great serpent: Ouroboros,*
> *show us again we are all*

And beneath the apse, the crypt. Humus rich with pomace
and wood, shed antlers, cellar stones buried, old-country
bones, then drift all the way down to limestone. The sun sets
and cool air settles in. The new crescent moon is an arc of
a spiral hanging silently over the resonating choir, over the
buzzing apse and the slumbering crypt, up in the darkening
vault of the sky.

> *Praise be to the sun, and to the moon, and to the ten*
> *thousand things*
> *Praise be to disintegration, and to confluence, and to the*
> *recurrent image,*
> *as it once was, will be again, and ever by turns shall be:*
> *braid with no end*

From Tsimshian Mythology
The Bear Who Married a Woman

Once upon a time there lived a widow of the tribe of the
G·i-spa-x-lâ'°ts. Many men tried to marry her daughter, but
she declined them all. The mother said, 'When a man comes
to marry you, feel of the palms of his hands. If they are soft,
decline him; if they are rough, accept him.' She meant that
she wanted to have for a son-in-law a man skilful in building
canoes. Her daughter obeyed her commands, and refused
the wooings of all young men. One night a youth came to her
bed. The palms of his hands were very rough, and therefore
she accepted his suit. Early in the morning, however, he had
suddenly disappeared, even before she had seen him. When
her mother arose early in the morning and went out, she
found a halibut on the beach in front of the house, although
it was midwinter. The following evening the young man
came back, but disappeared again before the dawn of the
day. In the morning the widow found a seal in front of the
house. Thus they lived for some time. The young woman

never saw the face of her husband; but every morning she found an animal on the beach, every day a larger one. Thus the widow came to be very rich.

She was anxious to see her son-in-law, and one day she waited until he arrived. Suddenly she saw a red bear (*mes-ô'l*) emerge from the water. He carried a whale on each side, and put them down on the beach. As soon as he noticed that he was observed, he was transformed into a rock, which may be seen up to this day. He was a supernatural being of the sea.

Editors' Note:

The Tsimshian are an indigenous people of the Pacific Northwest Coast of North America.

wi-ćaŋ´-ḣpi

the stars

haŋ-ye´-tu-daŋ

night, the black bear

win uŋ

it is creeping

he-ḣa´-ka-ta-pe-żi-hu-ta

elk-medicine

Paul Prudence
Scholar's Rocks
The Inter-Animating Spirit of Mind & Matter

All around the world are scattered stones that contain tiny
kingdoms of petrified forests and model mountains. These
stones with their imagined societies of people (and their ani-
mals and strange beasts) await to do trade and form alliances.
In each rock you may find exotic gardens, the wrecks of
ruined palaces. towering pinnacles, encrusted cliffs and the
fluted battlements of medieval castles. Every space is over-
run by lichens, vines and strange herbs. That *scholar's rocks*
have been prized for their mimicry of tiny topographies of
Lilliputian beauty is well attested by the great collections
from the T'ang dynasty to present times. But even before
that era of great adoration these rocks had already weathered
their apparitions into the human imagination. The pre-T'ang
literature tells of strange rocks in wild places that took the
form of dragons, saints and even monsters. And the metaphys-
ics of the microcosm found an early apogee in the Emperor's[1]
magic monuments made entirely from these stones.

Erosion, whose secrets are occluded only by time itself, has been busy; slowly dissolving rough rock into miniature worlds. The flow of water (that fertile archetype of time itself) has worn tiny rivers and valleys into stone, copying those processes of the greater world. Time flows through water and time flows through rocks, transforming them into mirror-worlds by attrition. And with more time these tiny streams in stone are turned to caverns which burrow down into the foundations of our own subconscious worlds. These caverns and other sunless chambers are the perfect hideouts for the dreamt-up denizens of our inflamed imaginations.

Nature has summoned its blind forces to create a fractal dimension, for each rock is a replica that displays *all* the processes by which the world fully reveals (and comprehends) itself. As diminished echoes of the earth's own features, scholar's rocks offer us a foci for studying this sense of planetary introspection. Nature's 'that I am' is cast into solid conscious form in which geological recollections of a former world are made manifest. The ghosts of stratified histories cascade through time and leave their marks in rock as totems or as scripts, or as tiny worlds, complete.

Miniaturism & Dimensionality | Miniature Worlds

To enter these miniature worlds we must first descend to the surface of these rocks. And as our imagination lowers itself onto these tiny vistas we become unchained from the conventions of ordinary space-time; or at least we mould their conventions according to our whims. Minutes tick in micro-time or else obey the magnitudes of aeons. Space is measured as an inverse of its real dimensions. It becomes limitlessly vast in the mesa of the mind's eye. As the imagination falls through this nexus of scales it moves through the

blood-brain barrier of dimensionality. And as we approach
the event horizon of these colliding scales we may experi-
ence a momentary black-out and a split-second of journeying
made through darkness. We awake as castaways on a floating
island made of stone (that famous levitation trick gifted to
us by Magritte). Returned to our smallest selves we return
to the moment of our most potent imagination. We are free
to survey every inch of our newly won kingdom from any
vantage point. Our sense of agency is sharpened by the
fantasy of this newly unlocked liberty. The shrunken self has
spelunked through the optic nerve and our bodies are now
irrelevant. We are free to begin the great eye-brain expedi-
tion. Imagination – connecting worlds and connecting scales
– is readied for adventure. There is no limit to our gaze in
space as it burrows deeper through the spectra of visible
features. We become high on the drug of spatial convergence
for here in this looking-glass-world the potency of space is an
inverse to its dimensions.

By mimicking the greater landscapes from which they
emerge, scholar's rocks reference the complete archive of
geology. As lithic compression artefacts they act as keys to
a whole. These small replicas of larger prospects justify that
well worn maxim of connectivity and continuity, *as above
so below*. But by some odd equivalent, they also allow us
relinquish our ties to that trusted falsity, *the bigger picture*.
In this newfound province all rules are of our own making
and we are free to explore by foot or, by rejecting the rooted
tyranny of gravity, by wing. On first arrival it may appear that
we are the sole inhabitant of this island stone. But soon that
thought dissolves as its crags and scarps twist their forms
into living creatures.

Disembodied the lively eye darts swiftly and acrobatically
across the terrain, hugging the ground or viewing from mul-
tiples. It clambers, it flies and it spies from above. And is it

no coincidence that each night on earth our dreams are full
of such flighted manoeuvres as if in preparation for these
disembodied campaigns? The omnipotent eye can now view
from any perspective. It has night vision and limitless zoom.
It moves millimetres above the lithic canopy observing the
details. And in diving deeper to scan the fractal dimensions
its view is pierced by clusters of lens flares. Dots of light race
like tiny coronal mass ejections across the lens of the eye.
Dancing green epicycloids and red roulette deltoids have
become the iridescent emblems of this newly found super-
natural sight.

Probing deeper below the mulch of petrified leaves we
discover patchworks of lichens in various colours and small
groups of spores that dapple and daub the rock in infinites-
imal shades. *Graphis scripta* unfolds its secret writing over
the ossified bark of the foot of a tree. This lichen can be
linear or star-shaped or even take the form of tiny labyrinths
in writing. These tiny mazes-as-letters form natural ciphers.
This is metamorphism as cryptography as nature's inscruta-
ble scripts are encoded into rock. Sometimes *scripta's* glyphs
approximate animals or demons so that its lithic vocabulary
doubles as divinatory system. Eyes trace out oracles and
omens through its labyrinths of puzzles.

As we continue our descent through the chain of scales
we find ourselves spiralling backwards through the spectra of
time. In visioning the tiny we approach our earliest memo-
ries. All experiences of miniaturising converge us towards a
common reference: mossy forests and mushroom shelters;
lawns with vast societies of ants and leaves that mimic great
barques in rivers of rain. The rewinding of time by this con-
traction of space returns us to half-remembered inklings of
a former life. And perhaps if we keep reducing the scale and
rewinding the tape eventually we may need to reborn. Time
and space – the fulcrums of our invention – attenuate each

other at their own pleasure and dance exotic shapes of contraction and expansion. Time runs faster in some parts but slower in others so that space is transformed into a hyperbolic construction. And what if our miniaturised self loses its way to trespass the periphery of this tiny dimension?

The vertiginous descent into the tiny can only go so far. Imagination falters as it approaches the event horizon of microfication. And as with Eames's *Powers of Ten* the vivid outlines of figures and forms eventually disintegrate into a fuzz of noise. Like the grain of a film magnified we are thrown into a storm of meaningless chaos without anchor. We have exceeded too many levels of recursion and have become removed from any reference to scale. The force of reduction rebounds us back off into space. But luckily for us any adept of miniaturisation is also the master of gigantism. And since both the tiny and the gargantuan displacements of self conform to the common seam of a disembodied continuum our reversed migration through space leaves us unscathed. In the distance the receding rock creates a new species of smallness as we view it from afar, deciphering its landforms as the pictograms of a map. Though our agency is lost to the distance we gain new perspectives because *that* distance subdues and dilates time. And so the serrations in stone, that once defined the crenulations of miniature fortifications, now sign the coastline of an ancient Tethys surging towards its future state. Landforms flutter and flow in intensive time-lapse as an invisible slowness is brought into light. We witness, for the first time, the metamorphic intent of geology as it boils its forms into the language of geographical history. Earth, that grounded symbol of fixed solidity seems ephemeral and vaporous — a liquid globe of shifting patterns that vindicate those who champion clouds as the model from which to study the earth in formation.

On earth we relinquish control to fate by imagining

greater beings controlling us like the pieces of a chessboard. Gods look down upon us and see us as their pawns, their miniature playthings. As slaves of scale we yearn for freedom from that fate. Scholar's rocks grant us escape so that we might find even smaller denizens and become *their* gods. The tendency to miniaturise the world, then, is allied with the impulse to escape it. There is a famous story of a Chinese painter[2] who disappears into the landscape he has painted. Stepping into pictures and stepping through dimensions is a revelatory act of transformation. It is an occult transition from consensual physics, an escape from the society of material dominion.

Note: To best effectively miniaturise space, one must be the lone surveyor of their kingdom. A world delicately suspended in the imagination is prone to distraction, or worse, threatened by the invasion of that most invasive of species — another's subjectivity.

The Scripts of the Cloudstones

A Jiansu dreamstone, a Yinde cloudstone, a fog-remnant-stone pulled from Lake Taihu — these are stones as frozen clouds or fossil scripts floating in shrouds of mist. Crammed with a webwork of curves — the enmeshed ascenders and descenders of an asemic cursive; these stones form a numinous cloud calligraphy. The negative spaces enclosed within their glyphs create an inverse prayer matrix for the rendering of a hollow-earth invocation. This is a writing as visionary topocosm where geology and writing are baked into a single codex. And is it not apt that imagination weathers its perception of stone to resemble the most archetypal of apophenic forms — the cloud? As children of a larger group of phantom forms both stone and cloud are mirrors to each other's

transmutability. Both encapsulate (and symbolise) the larger
class of dreamed-up forms. Like clouds, rocks reject percep-
tual fixity. Their continually shifting forms and textures are
ever keen to snatch their prizes from the eager void.

And if we speed up the choreography of geology by an
impossible factor what we will see are shapes that move
like clouds; twisting, transforming, evanescing. From this
we know that the Earth in formation can be understood by
observing the sky. Taoists and geologists, united in their
common awe of temporal boundaries, have long since
sensed that connection between cloud and stone. They
connect the things that form in instants with things that
form through aeons. They embrace the circularity of these
durations through meditation or in the field. They see clouds
and stones as tokens of a deeper continuum. Students of
the earth (and those who find themselves disembodied by
geology) are content with this extended space of durations.
They are in commune with stones and find community with
the clouds. In lithic meditation (or deep time introspection)
they are brought towards a totality of timeless material
indivisibility.

> Disciples make yourself exactly like the limitless ether,
> from yourself, from your senses, dissolve your souls,
> annihilate yourselves and surrender your temporal Soul
> —Chang Tzu

In Taoist tradition clouds represent the indifference a sage
aims to gain towards the body or the physical manifestation
of the world. They represent a kind disappearance that he
must attain. They symbolise the path to annihilation and
the sacrifice he must make in renouncing his mortal being.
The apposite stone then registers an uncanny counterpoint
to the endless duration of deep time and positions the body

as palpably insignificant to the point of omnipotence in
the redeeming power of ineffable presence. In her extraor-
dinarily epigenetic deep-time meditation on the geological
formation of the British Isles, Jaquetta Hawkes returns often
to the image of clouds, tapping into their forms and motions
as a way to connect with, and describe, otherwise incommu-
nicable ideas of geological consciousness and memory. Her
powerfully poetic passages invoke a timeless prehistory: 'The
clouds are all around me ... this luminous but impenetrable
envelope of greyness. It smothers not only all observation
but all thought. I am conscious of nothing but conscious-
ness, held here on a rock and engulfed by chaos'.[3] Hawkes's
receiver is not tuned to a biological timescale but to prehis-
torical geological memory. Like Taoists she meditates herself
towards the stone's inner essence and finds a way to access
its solid state memory that has somehow left its mark in the
stores of human consciousness.

The spiritual impulse to transcend the body marks a
special aspect of mind. The urge to commute beyond the
flesh finds focus in the alien shapes of geology that, them-
selves, transcend the flow of time. If clouds symbolise human
ephemerality, then rocks affirm the limits of human agency.
And this is why both clouds and stones have found their way
into the collective unconscious as symbols for our deepest
metaphysical questions on the nature of impermanence and
the paradox of time.

Hydrodynamic Writing

Some scholar's rocks are etched with such an abundance
of arcs and dots that they form a dense plane of kinetic
hieroglyphs. Like the magical scripts of Tobey or Michaux,
this writing floats in space like charged electricity or the

persisting trails of ionised particles. Liquefied ligatures suggest the flow of water: the true data visualisations of fluid dynamics. The lobes and eyes of the letters contain little ponds and in these apertures you may hear the faint sound of reverberating drips. This turbulent notation of hydro-graphic scrawls is pure-form writing. Water as a writer of scripts competes only with the clouds. And as Taoists know all too well (and as if to mock their own hands) the message it writes in rocks is always the same: 'you cannot do better then me'.

Conceived by this invisible hand of rheology, the ripples and whorls may sculpt the rock into an image of what? An image of *itself*. As time wears on, the stone becomes its own caricature, refining its own form by forcing the flow of water into echoes of its future shape. Feedback curves reverberate through the liquid-memory space, propagating themselves as sculptural carrier waves. Erosion has become an echoloca-tion system slowed the point of never receiving back its pro-jected signal. This is attrition as geophysical solipsism. And as the decades roll by the same mantra is repeated, re-writ-ten so that each twist in flow and turn in tide is recorded and remembered with a groove or line. Small shifts in flow amend and revise the annotations so that stone evolves a portrait of its own formation.

The jagged striations that contour some stones (those pencil lines that notate the diminishing echoes of each stone's form) repeat towards a proposed infinity and project a scheme towards its future shape. These sinuous lines etched by currents are cryptic tidal almanacs and memorials to each diurnal pull – the wax and wane of a lunar gravity consigned to lithic memory. And who can say? Perhaps all rocks contain a memory of some ancient phase or recall the tangle of some distant cosmic path. Somewhere held captive in a stone a secret astral trajectory is waiting to be known.

Algorithms & Manifolds

Erosion never takes time to rest and the sharp edges of some irregular rocks finally become so rounded as to suggest the complex forms of an algorithmic ornament: the crystalline structures of Byzantine geology razed from a Gothic Atlantis. Scaled, worn and scraped, these wrecked architectons of nature have been iterated beyond all ordinary dimension into mathematical caricatures of their former shapes. Coefficients in flow sculpt the stones into volumetric forms and exotic surfaces; the manifolds of crenulated bastions and castellated ruins.

A few accrue the forms of tiny terrains with spike-like growths. Palaces and palisades reside within these miniscule Balinese dimensions. Occasionally microorganisms have been allowed to collaborate in the micro-city spread. The turvey topocosm of minute terraces creates subspaces within this Garden of Eden configuration.[4] Iterative mosses map their territories over cubo-futurist facades in irregular tessellations. Bacterial colonies create radial diffusions. The rippling force of water has created tiny mountain peaks and fanning alluvial terrains. Dendritic spines elongate to form tiny skyscrapers – but the isometric view is flattened into a fractal flatland. An urbane sprawl of structures locked in place with precise (space-filling) intelligence. Proliferating textures imply a drama of multiplicities, city building and early forms of life decrypting the vectors of their own evolution. These mineralogical models of a reductive infinity are prized by mathematicians as much as metaphysicians. Pancomputationalists (and object-orientated geologists) have seen these calculations in stone so many times before. They know their shapes by heart. They see in each rock a single archetype; a seed, or prototype for the invocation of any rock. They see each rock as a single output from that larger program. Of course, nature has its own peculiar whims in computing forms that mimic its greater features and often makes 'mistakes'. Computations stutter and generate momentary glitches in natures own rendering system. Corrupted iterations output exotic reproductions. But nature has no thirst for the ideals of perfection. Nature adds nothing nor takes anything from its programs and its conditionals are never faulty. Each imperfection is a secret intention and clever ruse.

Strange Offerings

Nature is visible Spirit; Spirit is invisible Nature
—Friedrich Wilhelm Joseph Schelling

Through a process of attrition, nature has fashioned stones as strange offerings to the human imagination. With their landscapes and cloudscapes, and their nebulous writing. These figures in stone bind an arc between our proclivity for pattern recognition and our mythological imagination. They commune with the deep memory bank of human experience and expose this connection as a higher intention — a gift to us from the Earth itself. The things we see in stone have a habit of reflecting the cultural zeitgeist. They become talismans and totems of unnamable urges and the sublimated shapes of common obsessions. Our desires find shape in their curves and our dreams can be divined from their outlines. And so the collective imagination is forever being replenished by the occultations of deep-time, as its forces shape these intelligible forms.

That nature has devised a way to create clever facsimiles should be no surprise for it has also fine-tuned the equipment required to perceive them. A symbiotic flux occurs between the vision and the object of envisionment (the rock). That transaction creates a gradient of consciousness that transcends the conventional boundaries of biology and geology; a diffusion through the bio-mineral community sufficient for the dispersal of visions and myths. And though these visions live within the imagination, their pantheistic resonance transcend both body and spirit. Human consciousness secretes its spectres into stone as geology etches back its spirit into our collective imagination.

Sometimes the image beamed from rock to eye emerges as a ghost of its own intention. Imagination diffuses what is perceived with what it has projected so that the perceived and projected collide to form a layer of vivid connotation. This is the *inter-animating sprit of mind and matter* where biological and mineral kingdoms collude, where their inter-penetrating vectors are energised into a single field. (Meta) morphic resonance has opened a two-way transmission line so that geology can send messages to us in stone. The messages are mineralised into minds and in the marble patterns of neural pathways.

The transcendence of flesh through rock marks a special place in human consciousness. Against the immensity of geological time humans are sublimely insignificant. Paradoxically then, this creates a deeper sense of conscious connectivity with a continuum that exists outside of time and space. It returns us to a time undifferentiated (placing us at all points along time's endless thread) and at a point in space where no lines exist between each class of thing. But though these stones may seem fixed in the now-and-forever they too will eventually be erased by the surprises of time. Their figures and phantoms are doomed to be returned to rivers and onwards to oceans, or to be turned into dust for the replenishment of mountains. And pilgrims will be surprised to find the images of their gods and their scripts shattered and then reformed in this perpetual cycle of lithic transmigration. This is the constant shuffling of mythology, story and text through the landscapes that surround us into the landscapes of our imaginations. This is the cycling of rocks into mirror-forms of our own subconscious stratum.

What is to be found beyond the solemn subterfuge of these superficial visions? Perhaps our deep attraction to these phantom forms clue to us a deeper meaning. Psychologists will tell us that we see forms in clouds and stones because our brains evolved visual networks fine-tuned for survival. And that these shifting illusions are shaped by the rumbling afterglow of a hardwired system that long ago ceased to be a necessity. The networks continue to forge pictures, as if perpetually agitated by the flicker of noise, in the unstoppable laboratory of the imagination. And if these forms in stones invoke the figures of ancient scripts or superstitious imagery then they must also belie a deeper contract. The evolutionary circuits have unwittingly (or intentionally) created a substrate for a special kind of inner reflection. They have built a machine for reconnection; a system for recoupling our distanced selves by fusing our inner and outer worlds. Scholar's rocks are portals to the molten mantles of the psyche and all its dreamt-up denizens. And best of all these visions are suggested to us by nature — our imaginations' natural, and most honest, collaborator.

Notes:

1   Emperor Huizong of Song (7 June 1082–4 June 1135).

2   Wu Daozi (680–c.760), also known as Daoxuan, was a Chinese painter of the Tang dynasty.

3   *A Land*, Jacquetta Hawkes (1951).

4   In a cellular automaton, a Garden of Eden is a configuration that has no predecessor. John Tukey named these configurations after the Garden of Eden in Abrahamic religions, which was created out of nowhere.

Penelope Shuttle
Retrieved Data (Excerpts)

I send my thought
by an under-land route
from one end of the county
to the other
cavern by cavern

my thought travels via
the subterranean sublime

*

cobweb maps
of the five shadowy regions of Ancient Britain

*

red ruins of an abbey
in the Vale of the Deadly Nightshade

*

drift light
of the long evening

*

the day-time bat of St Devereaux
ghosting across the nave

*

nine-fingered monkey
cut into the arid plains of Peru
complete proof of eternity

*

a short history of the moon:
elephants, horses, and mystical beasts
prancing and capering
through clouds and flames,
indigos and ochres of moonshine

*

oak for the charcoal
hawthorn for kindling the hearth fires
a silver hawking whistle
violets from Keats' grave

iron age mirrors of great beauty,
incised on the obverse with spirals and crescents

*

bones of
goshawk
mallard pintail
rockdove rook
common scoter
goldfinch buzzard
jackdaw hedge-sparrow
crane raven
jay goose

great beauty
of their bones

*

sleep carries me round the world
all through the nine-day week
through forgetting and not-forgetting
past the shadow-builders
and into morning's *wake-up* of rain

From Southern African Folklore
The Great Star ǃgā́unū, which, singing named the Stars

ǃgā́unū, han̄ hā̱ ə̀ä ě ₁kuátten̦ ǃkérri; hé tíken ē̱, hǎ
lkē̱ ě̱ ǃgā́unū, ī̃; ŏ han̄ ttā ₁₁kǎ ti ē̱, hǎ ₁kǐ hā ā,
ǃkwiten̦ǃkwityǎ ₁kuǎ₁kuátten̦ lkéï₁kéï, ŏ hǎn̄ [   ] ttā
₁₁lkǎ tǐ ē̱, hǎ ₁kí ē̱ ǃkèrri. Hé tíken ē̱, hǎ ǃkwiten̦-
ǃkwiten̦ ₁kuǎ₁kuátten̦ ₁kéï₁kéï, ī̃. He tíken ē̱ ₁kuǎ-
₁kuátten̦ ₁kǐ hě̱ ₁kéï₁kéï, ī̃; ŏ hǐn̄ ttā ₁₁kǎ tǐ ē̱, ǃgā́unū
ǃkǐ ā ǃkwīya hě̱ ₁kéï₁kéï. Han̄ [   ] hā̱ ǃkùtten̦, ŏ hǎ
ǃkwì ₁kuǎ₁kuátten̦ ₁kéï₁kéï. Hǎn̄ kǎ: '₁₁X̣whāī', ŏ
₁kuǎ₁kuátten̦ ē̱ ‡eññttau; hǐn̄ ē̱, hǎ ddā hě̱ ā ₁₁X̣whāī;
hé̱ kǎ ₁nāī₁nāīn, hǐn̄ ē̱, ě̱ ₁₁X̣whāī.

Hé̱ tíken [   ] ē̱, ₁₁gǎŭX̣ŭ ₁₁nāū, he̱ ₁kuǎ₁kuáttā ssųe̱n̄-
ssųe̱n̄ ǃX̣ųŏn̄nĩyā, hǎn̄ ɔaúki tǎ hǎ ssě ₁₁nǎ̱₁₁nǎ̱ ǃkāūX̣ŭ;
tǎ, hǎ ‡en-na, tǐ ē̱, ǃgáuë ě̱, ŏ ₁₁X̣ehāī yǎ [   ] ttén̄
ǃX̣ųŏn̄nĩyā. Hǎn̄ ₁kŭ ǃkūīten; tǎ, hǎ ₁kǐ ₁₁ϑkoeń, he̱
₁kuǎ₁kuátten̦; hiń ē̱, hǎ ǃkɔ̀ä-ssě hě̱; ŏ hǎn̄ ttā ₁₁kǎ tǐ
ē̱, hǎ ‡eñ-nǎ, ti ē̱, ǃgáuë tǎ ₁kuǎ₁kuátten̦ ē̱.

Told by Dĩäǃkwā̱īn

Orthographic Notes:

Some of the graphemes and diacritical marks from the source material could
not be replicated, and have therefore been approximated.

₁	dental click		ǃ	cerebral click
₁₁	palatal click		X̣	aspirated guttural
ɔ	strong croaking sound		ϑ	gentle croaking sound
~	nasal		^	rough, deep

!gáunū, he was formerly a great Star; therefore, his name
is !gáunū; while he feels that he was the one who formerly
spoke (lit. 'called') the Stars' names; while he [   ] feels that
he is a great one. Therefore, he called the Stars' names.
Therefore, the Stars possess their names; while they feel that
!gáunū was the one who called their names. He [   ] for-
merly sang, while he uttered the Stars' names. He said
'ǁχwhāī' to (some) Stars which are very small; they are
those of which he made ǁχwhāī; their small, fine ones are
those which are ǁχwhāī.

Therefore, [   ] the porcupine, when these Stars have, sit-
ting, turned back, he will not remain on the hunting ground;
for, he knows that it is dawn, when ǁχwhāī has, [   ] lying,
turned back. He returns home; for, he is used to look at
these Stars; they are those which he watches; while he feels
that he knows that the dawn's Stars they are.

Translated by Wilhelm Bleek

Editorial Note:

> Bleek uses the term 'Bushman' to refer to the aboriginal people(s) of southern
> Africa, but the label is problematic, reflecting a certain European colonial per-
> spective. For a full discussion of this, and other terms such as 'San', see Robert
> Gordon, *The Bushman Myth*, 1992. According to Bleek, the narrator of this
> story 'came from the Katkop Mountains, north of Calvinia'.

Peter Mark Adams
Star Axis, New Mexico / Reflections

35.2644° N – 105.0870° W

Deus asked: 'How shall all things be as one, and yet each retain its divinity?'
And Night answered: 'Cast a net of infinite Aether around the sky,
encompass the boundless earth, the vast depths of the sea,
and all the circling signs of the heavens.
And when you have bound them,
lock them with a golden chain.'
—Orphic Fragments, 165–166.

Stellar time, that reckoning drift,
with all its unfathomable periodicities,
is rendered earthbound once more,
its belly impressed
upon the land to reveal

architectonic forms, emergent as
quarried sandstone, granite-capped shards;
blending with the natural contours of the mesa,
their exacting shapes
bestir ancestral memory to

bestow: visions of aeonic cycles,
those lost civilisations, the fleeting footfalls of myth;
whose fabulous creatures form
the dream-like tissue of stellar lore
anchored in the land.

Should we no longer feel
the pervasive, all-penetrant impress of the stars
upon these sensuously textured contours
or succumb to their enchantment
we would, indeed, be adrift in time; for

how remarkable it is that
these sky-sculpted memorials enjoin
our participation in some
indefinable and infinitely larger
pattern to which we naturally aspire.

A pattern sensed rather than seen,
amplified by these, the most intricate of geometries,
continues to proclaim the cycle of lives,
the eternal recurrence of spirit,
to a waiting world.

Edward Step
On the Rowan

The word Rowan is one of the most interesting of tree-
names, and connects the still-existing superstitious practices
of our northern countries, not only with old Norsemen, but
with the ancient Hindus who spoke the Sanskrit tongue.
The word is spelled in many ways which connect it with the
Old Norse *runa*, a charm, it being supposed to have power to
ward off the effects of the evil eye. In earlier times runa was
the Sanskrit appellation to a magician; *rûn-stafas* were staves
cut from the Rowan-tree upon which runes were inscribed.
Until quite recently the respect for its magical properties
was shown in the north by fixing a branch of Rowan to the
cattle-byre as a charm against the evil designs of witches,
warlocks, and others of that kidney. In this connection we
may quote also from Evelyn's *Sylva*. He says: 'Ale and beer
brewed with these berries, being ripe, is an incomparable
drink, familiar in Wales, where this tree is reputed so sacred
that there is not a churchyard without one of them planted

in it (as among us the Yew); so, on a certain day in the year, everybody religiously wears a cross made of the wood; and the tree is by some authors called *Fraxinus Cambro-Britannica*, reputed to be preservative against fascinations and evil spirits; when, perhaps, we call it *witchen*, the boughs being stuck about the house or the wood used for walking-staves.'

Among the numerous names of the Mountain Ash are Fowler's Service (or Servise, from *Cerevisia*, a fermented drink), Cock-drunks, Hen-drunks (from the belief that fowls were intoxicated by eating the 'berries'), Quickbeam, White Ash (from the colour of the flowers), Witch-wood, and Witchen. Quickbeam is an allusion to the constant movement of the foliage, quick being the Anglo-Saxon *cwic*, alive. Witch-wood and Witchen are also forms of cwic.

ṡuŋ

the large feathers of birds' wings

wa-ḣpe'-pe-żi-hu-ta

leaf-medicine

wa-zi'-ya-ta

at the pines, the north; the pole star

wo'-wa-hde-ćë

a twitching, an omen

Jake Crist
Protean Étude

> *...glimpses that would make me less forlorn.*
> —Wordsworth

The creekbed rocks surface like phocine scalps.

A white froth circles each tonsure,
Dissipates downstream. On either bank, slopes
Of snowy trillium – yellow anthers
Nearly sparkle in a shade of sugar
Maple and beech. Half-submerged in that rich
Carpet, fallen trunks like alligators
Seem almost imperceptibly to inch
Toward the creek.

         In the time it takes to twitch,
Every echinoderm and cephalopod,
Snail and clam, quickens and lifts from the clutch
Of the Ordovician limestone bed.

Wind swishes on the scene, a surreal word
Whispered to the water by the sealherd.

Jay Merill
The Four Winds

My name is Uchu and I was born in the north of Peru. A mountainous region. It was not a happy childhood. My mother and father were always in disagreement about things. Lately they had started shouting at one another and this frightened me. Then my father left home and we were very poor. I was the eldest and my mother took out all her anger and her despair on me. To travel away and never look back was something I longed to do. And I used to think the best thing in the world for me would be to journey on and on without ever revisiting the past. What I wanted most of all was to forget. By the time I was sixteen I'd come to believe I was destined to be a travelling man but maybe this was a stage I had to pass through in order to see more clearly and reach a positive state of mind. For a while though it did seem as if this were the right way to go; the only chance I'd have to make progress in my life.

Now I'm a few years older I think that to travel is perhaps

not what I thought it was. I already see the need I'd had was
a form of desperation. Which means this would not be a way
forward but more of a dragging back. The energy produced
would be all wrong for truly forging ahead and I believe now
that in the past it has pulled me down. Yes, if anything it
pulled me down. I do not blame myself for I had very little
knowledge of the way things work. But sometimes in life a
chance will open up before your eyes and when it does you
should take it for it is a magic moment and won't appear
every day. If you see such a window of opportunity you must
climb right in, though at first you may feel a little afraid as it
may be quite different from what you'd been looking for.

I have been lucky, for just such a chance has brought
me to the province of Huancabamba to meet with José, a
respected medicine man who resides there. He is seeking
an assistant and wonders if this could be something for me.
We've had many talks together since I came here and I find
we have a certain harmony of vision. Like José I am aiming
at going forward in my life in a way which is good for me
and good for the universe at the same time. But I have not
yet arrived at the point where I can imagine assisting others
in their quest for advancement of the self and this is where
we differ. José is not fazed by my lack of inspiration about
the development of others. He says that before such a step
can be envisioned it is necessary to first look at one's own
individual self.

After discussion between us over several days José pro-
nounced I was moving on the right path and I felt pleased
and gratified but I pointed out to him that I did not know
what the right path actually was. He laughed and said I must
not trouble about that at present but that we would speak of
this idea, and many others, over time. Don José has asked
me if I feel I could be happy to work with him as his assis-
tant and I tell him there is nothing I should like more and

that I hope I will prove to be a good one and that things will work out. He tells me not to worry and says that all will be as it is and we will glance from time to time to see how it is going and we will continue to have many talks. There are two other young men here already, both working as assistants to the maestro. Could I be in their company on a daily basis without experiencing any difficulty? I wonder if I could fit in.

I have to ask myself if I'm really ready to give up on the kind of life I'd planned. I had seen most clearly that to travel was my destiny and yet here I am thinking of making a commitment which would involve me being solely in one place.

José says it is best for me to not ponder too much at this stage and to just accept. Grow the big heart and with it will then come a time for expansion of the thoughts. I think he's telling me to go with the flow for the present and to reflect where this is leading me at a later stage. And maybe he is right. Or one would not be able to take a step forward. He tells me to breathe in deeply before I tackle each day. To breathe, and at the top of each breath to taste the air. He tells similar things to Ernesto and Videl, the two other assistants. We take his words very seriously. Don José is the maestro *curandero*. Many listen to him and feel better than they would have done in a hundred thousand lifetimes otherwise. So I try to accept that part of me still feels it is necessary to journey on through the world and another part of me is tempted to remain in Huancabamba. There is less cohesion in this conclusion than I'd have wished but seeing this gives me a giddy sensation that is not unpleasant. It makes me feel as though I could do anything.

The truth is that I'm still inexperienced in many ways, and my *curandero* sees that and does not expect more. The uncertainty laps round me as a lake would. I'm in the centre of the swirl. José waits to see if I will swim. There is no pressure anywhere. I will do this, or that. And the other two with me. They are just, like me, learning to breathe. This is exhilarating. Don José is not down on us expecting we should know this and should know that so we don't try to pretend to him or to ourselves, or to anyone, that we are bigger than we are. It feels good to be as I am myself, now at this moment. No bigger and no smaller than that. I explode and re-ignite with what I am. It's all I have. I see my feet at the end of my body, I see my two arms. Don José is showing how to be satisfied with yourself in the present. And if you are able to go with that you will make it possible to move forward. Just by carrying on doing what you do. Yes, I am learning to breathe.

Ernesto is a college student who is taking a year out. He's doing a course in psychotherapy and wants to learn about all methods of healing. To provide a wide background so that insights will come to him later on, he says. Videl is an older man who has just had his thirtieth birthday. He tells us he wants to expand the horizons of his thought and that's what made him come here as an assistant to the maestro *curandero*. They ask about me and I say that I had always seen myself as a travelling man and when I was on my travels I made a good friend, Daniela, a very special person. She was also a friend of José and she was the one who put me in touch with him. I say that I do not know what path I am now travelling on but don José said to me that it was the right one and I trust to his words in my time of uncertainty. Videl says in reply that *curanderismo* may be in itself a journey, though perhaps of a different kind from the one on which I was formerly embarking. I think about this and on instinct believe that he may be right. I can see Ernesto is also thinking about Videl's words as his face has taken on a look of concentration. At last Ernesto nods his head. From this I realise that the three of us are in some agreement. Emotion surges in me. This is the moment when I first feel I may belong here, in this new and to me still strange world.

We are busy. Many practical skills are to be learned and we must apply ourselves so that we become comfortable with all necessary tasks. This will be the best basis upon which to build. Awareness of other dimensions will follow on in their own time, in an organic and natural way. José tells us this and though in our lives as yet we have never had such an experience all three of us sense there is wisdom in his words. In a short while pilgrims will come here. Many seek help from the *curandero*. As the days go by I look forward to the arrival of those in need and of seeing how the maestro will be able to direct and help people in their quest for life changing illumination.

Don José takes us three assistants out to Las Huaringas which is not too far away from where we are placed. We walk into the mountains of Huaman for the first time in the early evening. All day we have been waiting for this visit to these sacred lakes, and our expectations run high. Round Laguna Negra we see giant reeds and spiked plants and there is a curious swishing as of ghostly branches at our approach. Later we find it was the hasty diving into water of Amazonian frogs and other small reptiles at the sound of our bodies pushing through the bamboo stems. Birds too rose up quickly or called warnings to one another from the branches of overhanging trees. Toucans and also the relojero bird we sighted watching us from bushes above. Videl was our bird expert and there were species we saw that even he could not identify.

Here at the lake we are to collect the wild herbs which grow in abundance. We must search through tall grasses and undergrowth, we must examine the base of rocks, and hunt through the muddy areas. Then wade into the shallow parts of the lake itself. Don José shows us which herbs and wild flowers it is necessary to pick. He talks about the various plants as we proceed, and later on at home explains how they work to assist healing; how we are to use them to create concoctions for imbibing and also for putting into amulets. He tells us which will give protection against the sorcery of the *brujos* and *brujas*. I feel greatly favoured to be selected as a pupil of this learned shaman.

Also we must make good the huts where the pilgrims will reside. These are wooden structures around one courtyard at the rear of don José's house. There are a few repairs to attend to and some tiling which needs to be done in the bathrooms as well as the re-staining of the wooden walls. More excitingly, we handle the *artes* with which don José will be doing divining on behalf of those who come. There are stones and quartz and the fragments of some green striated rock, besides an array of colourful shells, other objects I cannot fathom at all, plus the collar bone of a tapir. In addition to these there are some chunks of ore, and several antiquated seed pods which look to be about one hundred years old at least. These are the tools which don José will use to reach the reticent spirits of those who seek but who have not yet found.

The most sacred duty we have at this stage is learning an acquaintance with San Pedro. There is a hush of respectful silence when the maestro first introduces this cactus to us.

'This plant is our great and reverenced teacher,' don José tells us, his tone hushed. He holds the cactus firmly in his two hands. By this means he conveys to us the huge importance of San Pedro in the shamanic process. We three apprentices handle the plant with great care for we know it is at the centre of the universe we are approaching, and is vital to our instruction and also for the benefit of those who will come to this place for spiritual nurturing and enlightenment.

We are, José tells us, to imagine the Cosmos. The objects he has set before us on his *curandero's* altar will guide us to a correct way of perceiving it. We are to drift into the sacred sphere in our own time, at our own pace. There should be no competitive element to distract. For the truth that is present is between each spirit and the divine. We sit at a doorway; when we enter and what we discover is our very own. San Pedro is the bridge which will connect each of us to the sacred domain. On hearing these serious words spoken by the shaman we three students sit in a spirit of humble longing before him and the *mesa* of his representational world. Then we take in the mescaline offered to us and this is what we reach...

First of all sleep. It is as if I never have slept before in my lifetime. Never known what sleep was or could be. I fall into it like a heavy weight into water, causing a large splash. Then, nothing. I'm submerged. This all happens quickly but still it is a gentle process, nothing to faze anyone. It's a drifting out and away. From what once mattered and from all that inhibits now. I think of a journey; think of travelling. In a flash I see that I have looked on travelling as a means of necessary escape. But escape is not the real answer to anyone's needs. This comes to me as a sudden flare of white which does not go away but starts to form into a column which turns purple at the tip. How delicious is this sleep which has inside it the knowledge that I will wake up refreshed. I somehow receive the message that this is not the sleep of death but of life. This is its beauty and its strength. The drowsiness that takes me to the deeper levels is like a hot wind blowing into my face so that my eyes must close. There is a dreamy hazy look to things as my lids press downwards; a slight dizzy feeling. Later, on waking, Ernesto, Videl and I talk excitedly of the wonder of the sleep we have been through. Our experiences were very much the same we find. And that we all have undertaken this initial step is a bond drawn between the three of us. We are becoming like brothers. Except that real flesh brothers may not be so

close as those who are finding a common way of entering
this spiritual world. In the evenings we do up the huts in
which the pilgrims, when they arrive, will stay while they are
receiving instruction from the shaman. Or we accompany
don José to Laguna Negra to gather the wild herbs for his
preparations. And there is talk and good fellowship present
amongst us.

After the sleep comes a stirring vision. All the rich
colours that visit in dreams are spreading out in front of my
eyes now. Images hover, higher than me but reachable. Then
they settle, and then they become fused into one single form.
I see the mighty Cactus of the Four Winds. It is right there
before me in all its natural radiance. I can breathe only very
slowly now because of the awe. Too much breath would seem
like a disturbance. The Cactus glows and all the colours that
appear in dreams are present inside it. Everything else in
me is wiped away, the last to leave is thought itself. I am just
staring and drinking in the sight in front of me. My mind
rests as clean and open as my favourite shell in the maestro's
collection. Air flows through it and through the rest of me.
All is heightened now. The real has become unreal. The
Cactus that will teach me to find myself seems to be giving
off specks of golden light. I can hardly look at them they are
so bright and hot and potent. They draw tears from my eyes
which cloud everything. Until at last my eyes are aching,
aching. And then I can see nothing.

I'm aware of a tingling sensation. It fizzles on the tips of
my fingers, runs across my upheld hands and down my arms,
brought in by a wind of change. For the vision of San Pedro
has faded down to a blurred darkness now that what I see
is half obscured by mist. All my fingers, my two hands and
both my arms are becoming numb. I've never really pictured
heaven and so I can't quite put into words what I mean, but
I see a threshold before me. It is leading somewhere and

heaven is I think where. But before I reach it I may have to pass through life and death.

Now a sense of peace is with me. The tingling in my body is no longer present. I do not feel tired and therefore don't feel like sleeping. This is a different level of calm from what I've known. I am warm and soft and I do not notice my breathing and do not need to even consider it. That the breathing is happening somewhere is enough. I must have been lying down flat on my back for I become aware of myself rising up on one elbow and leaning there on the floor with the cosmos of the maestro right before me. My eyes light on three feathers which I did not previously notice. I understand that these are the feathers that will brush away pain. 'In a light fluttering movement they will alight onto you. You will feel them caress the skin of your body. When they are gone the weight of past hurt will be gone too. You will be as light as a feather itself is.' As I lie here, leaning on one elbow, vaguely conscious of Ernesto crouching to one side and Videl, kneeling down the other side of him, I hear the voice of José. It seems to be in the whole of the room. The thoughts I have just had I recognise as the words of the shaman working through me.

Don José is now taking up bones and stones and a short length of driftwood. It is weathered, this wood, and light with porosity. These *artes* he places with the feathers at the centre of the *mesa nortena*. I feel myself balanced between light and dark and yet detached from either. But I sense the mind of José close by, and also the spirit of San Pedro guiding him like a star at night. It seems that my mind and body are divided at this moment and may go their separate ways. My mind may rise up very high and I may watch my body lying, still leaning on one elbow, on the ground. I feel in touch with all things in nature and as though I am able to flow with them. Then I picture the wings which will take

me upwards. For, yes, I will go upwards, and yes I will fly.
Through time as well as across distance. I am an astral body
soaring through air. I belong everywhere and nowhere and
I can look down upon all on earth, including myself. I can
arrive anywhere I wish to be. It is so glorious to have this
sense of detachment about myself; from former cares; and
from this world. Although I am still lying leaning on one
elbow it is as if I am no longer on the floor. I am flying in the
four directions. First the powerful North draws me to itself,
then the dynamic South, thirdly the death-dark West. Finally
I am re-born from this into the pure-gold East. So, I have
journeyed to the four corners of possibility yet I have not
shifted from the place where I am.

The weeks run along with us apprentices assisting the
maestro in preparing for his curandismo practices, the
healing and ritual pathways along which he will negotiate the
souls of the pilgrims. He shows us how to cut into and slice
the four ribbed cactus, how to make the medicinal drink
from its flesh. We now prepare tobacco and the other plants
which also have been gathered for this purpose and for use
in the amulets. And we speak about the art of divination and
all the necessary elements which must go into the attainment
of this. I am becoming more and more familiar with the
histories of the *artes* and to recognise which space each pre-
cious object must occupy upon the *mesa*, and to understand
why. The cabins now look very smart and we are all proud
of the work undertaken to such good effect. Soon the first of
the pilgrims will be arriving.

In the evenings don José talks about the spirit in things.
Ernesto asks if he is referring to ordinary things or to cer-
tain special venerable objects alone. Don José tells us that
spirits reside in all things but that those with which we form
a special relationship are the ones which will be relevant for
our particular use. He says further that the master spirit of

San Pedro will guide us in the right direction to discover
what will draw our own spirituality to the fore. San Pedro,
says the maestro, will teach us like children, about the tools
we will need for the safe passage of the spirit from within
our own hearts, and about the spirits we must seek elsewhere
which will develop and enhance our own. This process is the
journey of journeys. I carefully consider his words.

Also during the evenings Videl plays his guitar for us and
sings some of the old traditional songs of the Andes which
he has been learning. This sets up a good atmosphere. I do
not recall ever in my life having a better experience than
sitting with these new like-minded friends in the room
where we take our recreation. And I think I have never truly
learned to relax and to give out before, and to be entirely
trusting of others and unafraid. The beginning of feeling bet-
ter about myself and everything around me which started to
happen when I was with Daniela and her friends in Yanque
has gone on to flourish here in Huancabamba. I think of
Daniela in particular with affection and am grateful to her,
and I will never forget that it was she who introduced me to
this estimable world which I had never before experienced or
thought to find.

It is now coming up to February and Enrico says he
would very much like to go to Carnival at Cajamarca as this
will happen just before the pilgrims are set to arrive here.
José asks Videl if he wishes to go also. But Videl wants to
stay where he is in meditation and repose for the time availa-
ble to him prior to the appearance of the guests. José says to
me why don't Enrico and I go together? And I could catch up
with some distant family members who live in the region. I
haven't seen them for quite a while, he reminds me. Would it
not be a pleasant interlude prior to the concentration of our
work later on, he asks. Enrico is enthusiastic, I at first am
not quite sure. Though José says, why not? To this I have no

answer. The idea I used to have about travelling relentlessly on and never revisiting the past has left a trace in me. I recognise it as the taste of fear. But...

'Why not go?' says don José in a voice both hard and soft. And I ask myself the same question.

'Yes,' I reply at last. And a shout of joy starts up in me when I have said the word, which feels like the unfolding wings of a bird. It is as if a mist has dissipated and I see clearly that I long for this.

There is a time when I discover within me what the maestro has said quite clearly was the aim. When I know I have arrived at the position which he was describing. Don José spoke of a flower opening and said it should be this way in the soul of a person. He told us about the significance of the number four in Andean cosmology, and of this I was already half aware. Well, I knew it a little at one level but now I have understood it at another. With the open benevolence of San Pedro I reach an altered state of mind, and I sit as my own small being but also as my vast cosmic self upon the floor beside the *mesa* of the maestro. In my mind I see that I am a giant and perfect four-petalled flower. I turn round and look at myself from every conceivable angle. And yes, it is so. Then as I sit and see, I enter and become the texture and the petals of this perfect bloom. And I exult in this blooming; feeling joy in my heart. The four petals, which also are myself, open in a slow and deliberate movement. It's like discovering the centre of the universe and the centre of your own heart in one and the same moment. And then I see that the universe and I are as one. Next I arise from the deep secret pivot of the flower and go up and ever up into the air of La Sierra. I do not stop but become as a gigantic bird with a vast wing span, flying in a single breath. Going higher, higher, until I am everywhere. You cannot now distinguish me from the clouds, from the blue; from the endless sky.

Here is the idea which has been forming slowly. The meaning of travel itself. I've undertaken a life-changing journey yet am exactly where I was at the beginning. This says to me you can go travelling without ever lifting your feet from the ground. For the greatest of life's journeys are the ones which travel between your soul and the world you inhabit.

Dan Beachy-Quick
Canto VII

Liv'd
    among aspen and pine liv'd some time
    in the bright moody summers among willow, maple, oak
        and the dogwood's three-petalled flower open and white
        that come July withers on the ivy dark

But if you have not liv'd a long life among the olive trees
        whose leaves shine sudden and sudden blink shut
you cannot feel the life within the word *glaukoris*
        you cannot see Athena's eyes
            beyond the bright-eyed epithet of Athena's eyes

the owl on the branch in the dusk stares out reading...

like silent letters in a word the mice live in the field...

From Klamath Folklore
List of Incantations

Yámash kiúksam shuî'sh, mû'ash, tyálamash, yéwash, slä'wîsh,
paíshash, lĕmé-ish, lúepalsh, któdshash, gulkásh.
Sáppas kiúksam shuísh, sháp'sam stutî'sh; yaína, wálidsh,
ktá-i sû-smaluatk, hä'nuash, yatî'sh, sámya-ush, é-ush,
wélwash, káwam, wäyá-lapsh.
Snáwedsh kiúksam shuî'sh, welékag, tsákiag, tsákiaga
tsû'yatyant; k"mutchä'witk: ḵó-idshi shuî'sh génti
kä'ilati.
Gû'tkaks kiúksam shuî'sh, gudítguls, shíllals, tátktîsh,
lulúlish, tiló-takna, tiä'mîsh.
Munána tatámnish kiúksam shuî'sh, kĕláyua, múkukag,
wáshlaag, gî'wash, tsásgai, tsáskaya wéash, kólta wéas,
Skélamtch, wályatska, kútch-ingsh, wán, ké-utchish,
witä'm, lû'k.
Yaúkal kiúksam shuî'sh, tchuaísh, tsásyībs, skólos, p"laíwash.
Ndukî'sh kiúksam shuî'sh, wítkatkish, tsíktu, tsántsan,
túktukuash, shkä', spû'm.
Wákwakinsh kiúksam shuî'sh, shpíu'hpush, skaúkush.
Ḵaḵan kiúksam shuî'sh, tsóks, tchiutchíwäsh, nä'-ulinsh,
shuä't.
Wíhuash kä'-ishalsh sháyuaksh kiúksam shuî'sh, kä'kak-tkaní
tsíkka, ḵalyals (ḵáls), tchíkass kshíkshnîsh, wuiplé-ush,
skúlä, tsísyîyî, tchä'-ush, núsh-tilansnéash, tsyä-utsyä'-
ush, póp-tsikas.

cont.

North wind has an incantation-song, south wind, west wind,
  east wind, gust of wind, cloud, thunder, lightning, rain,
  rain mixed with snow.
Sun has a *tamánuash*-song, mock-sun; mountain, rock-cliff,
  rocks-spotted, upright rocks, upright rocks (smaller),
  rocks in river, lake, water-spring, eel-spring, floating
  ice.
Woman has a *tamánuash*-song, old woman's spirit, little boy,
  little boy (restless); the old man: (is) an untoward song
  in this country.
Small-pox is an incantation, belly-ache, chronic sickness,
  pain, cramps, cause of sickness, hunger.
Mole has a *tamánuash*-song, ground-mouse, field-mouse,
  chipmunk, squirrel, weasel, weasel's young, otter's
  young, Old Marten, black marten, deer's claw, silver-
  fox, gray wolf, black bear, grizzly.
Bald eagle has a medicine-song, black vulture, a black night-
  bird, turkey buzzard, gray eagle.
Pigeon hawk has an incantation, small hawk, mice-hawk,
  little fishing-hawk, fish hawk, gray hawk.
Red-headed woodpecker has an incantation, spotted
  woodpecker, large black woodpecker.
Crow is a medicine-song, blackbird, 'snow-producer', black
  forest bird, sedge-cock.
Snowbird in [being a] snow-making expert is a conjurer's
  medicine, yellowish bird, a spotted night-bird, a
  mountain forest-bird, little forest bird, lark, *tsísyîyî*,
  yellow-hammer, 'rollhead', blue jay, drinking bird.

Kû'lla kiúksam shuî'sh, wéaks, náta, mpámpaktish, tsáolaks,
    mámak-tsu, kîlidshiksh, wá-u"htush, túiti, múläläk,
    póp-wäks.
Weíwash kiúksam shuî'sh, kû'sh, kúmal, tsákĕnush, tchákiuks,
    táplal.
Méhiäs kiúksam shuî'sh, yä'n, tsuám, tsû'lpas, tcháwash,
    kû'tagsh, tsálayash.
Wámĕnags kiúksam shuî'sh, kámtilag, wíssink, ḵé-ish.
Lä-a-ámbotkish kiúksam shuî'sh, wä'kätas, kóä, kía, skû'tigs;
    laḵí shuísham kó-ä.
Kínsh kiúksam shuî'sh, ámpuam lák.
Wû'kash kiúksam shuî'sh, wássuass, ktséämu, sä'l, waktä'lash,
    wá'hlas.
Wû'ns kiúksam shuî'sh, ktsík, sákuas, kî'sh; syī'l, k"nû'ks,
    ndû'ks, pála, kátchgal, sáwals.
Tánt wakî'sh kiúksam shuî'sh, shashtanû'lōls, wásh,
    shánhish, pápkas, stsá-usa wálks, lû'loks, slû'kops,
    slû'mdamd-wash.
Lû'baks, klêpki kiúksam shuî'sh, tsé-usam skû'tatk, tsé-usam
    tsúyätk, tsé-usam lä'sh, witkakísham lä's.
Kat"sitsutsuéas kiúksam shuî'sh, kat'hiáwash, lû'luks-
    skû'tchaltk, skû'ksam hä'kskîsh, hä'näsish.

Editors' Notes:

    The Klamath are an indigenous people from southern Oregon, in the United States of America.

    Square brackets have been added for clarity.

Red-headed duck has an incantation, mallard, little black
duck, small duck, red-eyed duck, black-and-white duck,
large duck, long-legged duck, young duck, shoveler-
duck, *póp-wäks*.

White goose is a doctor's medicine, swan, pelican, *tsákĕnush*,
a gray fowl, loon.

Trout is a conjurer's medicine-song, small sucker, large
sucker, *tsûlpash*-fish, a little sucker, minnow-fish,
salmon.

Black snake is a song-medicine, a black snake, garter snake,
rattlesnake.

'Never-Thirsty' is a conjurer's song, green frog, toad, lizard,
lizard ['chief of songs' toad].

Yellow-jacket is a conjurer's medicine, horse-hair.

Pond-lily seed is a medicine song, lacustrine grass, aquatic
grass, arrow reed, shaft-wood, pole-tree.

Dug-out canoe is an incantation, oar, fish-spear, harpoon;
otter-skin strings, rope, pestle, scoop, tobacco,
arrow-head.

Of sweat-house floor inside ladder is a conjurer's song,
outside ladder of sweat-house, excavation, rafter,
lumber, stick-hole, fire, cavity, remains of old
sweat-house.

White chalk, red paint are doctors' songs, *tché-ush*-dressed,
tché-ush-head-covered, *tché-ush*-feather, hawk's feather.

Snow-flake witchcraft is a doctor's song, hair-tying, in fire-
robes, spirit's walking-staff, conjurer's arrow.

Lady Gregory
Oisin's Laments (Excerpt)

Blackbird of Doire an Chairn, your voice is sweet; I never heard on any height of the world music was sweeter than your voice, and you at the foot of your nest.

The music is sweetness in the world, it is a pity not to be listening to it for a while, O son of Calphurn of the sweet bells, and you would overtake your Nones again.

If you knew the story of the bird the way I know it, you would be crying lasting tears, and you would give no heed to your God for a while.

In the country of Lochlann of the blue streams, Finn, son of Cumhal, of the red-gold cups, found that bird you hear now; I will tell you its story truly.

Doire an Chairn, that wood there to the west, where the Fianna used to be delaying, it is there they put the blackbird, in the beauty of the pleasant trees.

The stag of the heather of quiet Cruachan, the sorrowful croak from the ridge of the Two Lakes; the voice of the eagle of the Valley of the Shapes, the voice of the cuckoo on the Hill of Brambles.

The voice of the hounds in the pleasant valley; the scream of the eagle on the edge of the wood; the early outcry of the hounds going over the Strand of the Red Stones.

The time Finn lived and the Fianna, it was sweet to them to be listening to the whistle of the blackbird; the voice of the bells would not have been sweet to them.

Brian Johnstone
A Lock of Fleece

Bury me, he said,
the way old shepherds went
to meet their God.

Strangers to the church,
its doors were never darkened
while the flock had needs.

Sundays saw them always
in the hills, sheep and lambs
their congregation,

the ones that went astray
of more concern
than any hymns or psalms.

Where they broke bread
a place of dry stone dykes,
of styles and fanks.

How then to know,
when death defeated them,
that they were true to faith?

A lock of fleece
held tightly in the hand
when laid between the boards

enough to say this man
was never one to turn his face
away from God, say —

Look, a shepherd comes
to hills he only could imagine.
Now let him pass.

i-kaŋ'ye-taŋ-haŋ

on the river- or lake-side of an object

wa-na'-ġi

the soul when separated from the body

wa-se'

red earth, vermillion

na-ġi'-ya

to go to the spirit-world

James Goodman
Ends of saints

Budoc, huddled in the barrel of his birth,
drifts and spins on devil currents
for twenty years, sights land, strikes
the foreshore reef, splinters bone and timber,
bloodies rocks and pools.

*

Piran rolls his deadweight millstone up the angle of the beach
and there on the sand builds his chapel of sand
which becomes a dune marked by a millstone
that is bound in drifts of sand and marram grass,
and Piran prays and breathes only sand.

*

Tiny Ia, crosslegged on her ivy leaf, slides in
on the leaf-tide of a creek, slides out
again as the sea recoils, flips on a wave,
zigzags down through the darkening water
into the conger-pit of the deep estuary's cleft.

*

Gorran picks over the headland angles
of his surreptitious entrypoint.
Hampered by the torments of a devil wind
harried by a cliff of vicious gulls, he chokes in the
nitrate smear of their full misgivings.

*

Zennor births Budoc as she floats,
sends him off in a barrel to shore.
Her postnatal care is performed by the waves,
provisioned by the commons of the ocean —
the care deepens till there's no more light.

*

Neot drowns in the well-spring of his devotions
Mawes drops to the mauling of a too-bold seal
Dilic addles with the bad milk of her sister's cow
Cuby turns his face too often to the sun
Yestin bursts through the rot of the mineshaft's cap.

*

Mewan bearing weighty Austel on his back
slumps dead as his mentor-burden leans
to pick a campion from the hedge. His body
turns to granite, with tourmaline veins. Lizards
flick across his crouched and crooked monument.

*

Austel, faced by the open cast mine of his ambitions,
stumbles on a sharp and dash of gravel,
cascades like a jackdaw and breaks on a jutting water pipe
by the pit-sump. The little stream seeps red,
runs red into the v-shaped valley, sullies the bay.

Magda Isanos
Five Poems

Viață, Nu Mă Părăsi

Viață, nu mă părăsi în răsăritul acesta,
privește fruntea mea de pe-acum aurie.
Și aerul din cauza viitoarelor fructe
e rumen și plin.

Viață, încălzește puțin începutul acesta,
ascultă numele meu de pe-acuma sonor.
O pasăre zbura-n cea dintâi zi repetându-l,
și pomii ceilalți atunci mă luară de mână:
— Hai să-nflorim...

Tu nu mi-ai spus despre toamna frunzelor roșii,
tu nu mi-ai spus despre moartea copiilor,
nici pentru ce trandafirul sălbatic
râdea-n cimitir...

Life, Do Not Abandon Me

Life, do not abandon me to this dawn,
look how my forehead is already golden.
Even the air is bursting and pungent
because of all the fruits to be.

Please life, warm gently this beginning,
listen how my name is already echoing.
A bird was flying on the first day repeating it,
and the other trees then took me by the hand:
— Come, let us blossom...

You did not tell me about the autumn of red leaves,
you did not tell me about the death of children,
nor did you tell me why the wild rose
was laughing in the graveyard...

Întoarcere

Vor fi și-atuncea ierburi și zăpezi...
Tu, ochi, cum ai să rabzi să nu le vezi?
„Ba nu, mai pe-nnoptate-am să mă scol,
să dau livezii, stupilor, ocol,
să mângâi lemnul ușilor de-acasă
și păpușoii galbeni pe mătasă.

Dulăii vor veni să mă miroase,
cu boturile negre, somnoroase,
și gudurând spinările: 'stăpână,
de unde vii, că mirosi a țărână?'"

Homecoming

There will still be greenery and snow...
Eye, how can you bear not seeing it?
'Oh no, I will wake up when night comes,
and I will circle the orchards and the bee hives,
to caress the wood of doors from home
and the yellow corn husk dolls.

Wild dogs will come to sniff me,
with black, sleepy muzzles,
and, fawning with their bristling spines, greet me: "mistress,
where are you coming from that you smell of graveyard dirt?"'

Vis Vegetal

Vreau, suflete, să mă dezbar de tine
și să trăiesc ca pomii de pe vale,
cu flori în locul gândurilor tale,
o viață fără rău și fără bine.
Departe, într-o pădure de la munte,
când păsările toate-or face haz,
să mă trezesc cu soarele pe frunte
și lacrimile cerului pe obraz.
Și despletita ploaie să mă spele
de pulberea durerii de demult,
din care rădăcinile mi-am smuls,
iar nopțile să-mi dea cercei de stele.
Luna cea plină vreau s-o cumpănesc
mirată-n lanțul crengii ca pe-un cuib.
De raze și de sevă să mă-mbuib,
ca tot deasupra altora să cresc.
Atunci mi-oi face ferecate strune
din ramurile mele și-am să cânt
doar bucuria fragedă că sunt;
pădurea-n jurul meu o să s-adune.

Verdant Dream

I want, dear soul, to free myself of you
and live as trees live in the valley,
with flowers where your thoughts once grew,
a life without evil and without good.
Far away, in a mountain forest,
where all the birds would sing at once,
to wake up with the sun on my forehead
and with heaven's tears on my cheek.
I want the naked rain to wash me
of the dust gathered by the pain of ancient times,
the pain from which I pulled my roots,
and nights to gift me stars instead of earrings.
I want to ponder upon the full moon
astonished, nestled on the chain of a branch.
I want to drink all the sap and fill myself with rays,
so I can grow above everyone else.
And in that moment I shall force hidden strings
from my twigs and I shall sing
of nothing but the raw thrill of being:
all forest trees will gather round me.

Pomii Cei Tineri

Pomii cei tineri, în dimineaţa de marte,
unii lângă alţii au stat să se roage —
frunţile lor străluceau inspirate deasupra
pământului încă-n zăpezi.

Şi-n aerul în care nu erau zboruri,
pomii, ale căror umbre nu se născuseră,
cântau un imn pentru viaţă,
ca nişte oameni goi şi frumoşi ei cântau:

„Soare de-aramă, zeu popular printre plante,
 priveşte oastea noastră-ndrăzneaţă;
ici-colo aerul e rumen de tot printre ramuri,
că viitoarele fructe acolo vor sta...

Noi nu ne-nchinăm de fel şi nu plângem,
ci pregătim un loc cât mai înalt pentru cuiburi
şi pregătim o orgă de brazi pentru vânturi,
soare de-aramă, zeu totdeauna rotund...

cont.

The Young Trees

On the morning of March, the young trees
stood in prayer one next to the other —
their inspired crowns shining above
the ground still covered in snow.

And in the flightless air,
the trees, with shadows yet unborn,
were singing a hymn to life,
like beautiful naked people they sang:

'Bronze sun, loved god among the plants,
look at our daring legion;
here and there the air bristles between branches,
for that is where future fruits will be...

Our nature does not let us bow and cry,
but prepare a home for nests high up,
and an organ of fir trees for the winds,
oh bronze sun, ever round god...

Ni s-a povestit despre tine-n pământ,
când nu cunoșteam dimensiunile cerului;
ni s-a povestit despre tine-n leagănul cald.
Semințele-n somn visau că există colori,
roșu, albastru și gri, minunate colori.
Tu, peste frunțile noastre, soare, cobori.
Și noi vom da fructe, și noi vom fi hore de flori.
Gloria noastră toată-n vârf se presimte."

Și-un curcubeu pe deasupra tulpinilor strimte
cade vestind: nu moarte, desigur, nu moarte,
pomilor tineri în dimineața de marte.

We were told about you in the ground,
when we had not known the measure of the sky;
we were told about you in the warm cradle.
In sleep, our seeds dreamt that colours exist,
red, blue and grey, marvellous colours.
Sun, please descend upon our crowns.
And we will bear fruit, we will become a dance of flowers.
For all our glory is foretold by the canopy.'

So then a rainbow falls as a sign
above the narrow stems: no death, of course, no death at all
for these young trees on the morning of March.

Aş Vrea Un Basm

Aş vrea un basm, dar cine să mi-l spună
când a tăcut de-o vreme chiar si vântul?
E focul stins şi noaptea-i fără lună,
si muzei mele i-a-nghețat cuvântul.

Era o fată şi-un bunic bătrân;
erau povesti şi maci aprinşi în lunci;
parfum şi greieri ce cântau în fân —
şi-i mult de tot de-atunci.

Bătrânu-i mort acum, si buzele-i sunt mute.
El doarme-n sânul bunului pământ,
şi de-ar trăi, azi, cine să-i asculte
povața înțeleptului cuvânt?

A scârțâit o mobilă prelung,
şi vântul parcă plânge la fereşti —
neostenite clipele se scurg.

Nu-i nimeni să m-adoarmă cu poveşti.

I Wish For A Fairy Tale

I wish for a fairy tale, but who can tell me one
when even the wind has been quiet for a while now?
The hearth is cold, the night is without moon,
and my muse has fallen silent.

There once was a girl and an old grandfather;
there were tales and fiery poppies in the fields;
perfume and crickets singing in the hay —
but a long time has passed since.

The old man is now dead, and thus his lips are mute.
He sleeps in the bosom of mother earth.
But even if he were alive today, who would listen
to the cautions of his wise word?

The furniture creaks in long sighs,
the wind seems to be crying at my window —
tireless the moments are dripping.

There's no one here to tell me stories at night.

Translated from Romanian
by Christina Tudor-Sideri

Robert Hooke
Micrographia (Excerpt)

As in *Geometry*, the most natural way of beginning is from a
Mathematical *point*; so is the same method in Observations
and *Natural history* the most genuine, simple, and instruc-
tive. We must first endeavour to make *letters*, and draw *single*
strokes true, before we venture to write whole *sentences*, or
to draw large *Pictures*. And in *Physical* Enquiries, we must
endeavour to follow Nature in the more *plain* and *easy* ways
she treads in the most *simple* and *uncompounded bodies*, to
trace her steps, and be acquainted with her manner of walk-
ing there, before we venture our selves into the multitude of
meanders, she has in *bodies of a more complicated* nature;
lest, being unable to distinguish and judge of our way, we
quickly lose both *Nature* our Guide, and *ourselves* too, and
are left to wander the *labyrinth* of groundless opinions;
wanting both *judgement*, that *light*, and *experience*, that
clue, which should direct our proceedings.
    We will begin these our Inquiries therefore with the

Observations of Bodies of the most *simple nature* first, and
so gradually proceed to those of a more *compounded* one. In
prosecution of which method, we shall begin with a *Physical
point*; of which kind the *Point of a Needle* is commonly
reckoned for one; and is indeed, for the most part, made so
sharp, that the naked eye cannot distinguish any parts of it:
It very easily pierces, and makes its way through all kinds
of bodies softer than itself: But if viewed with a very good
Microscope, we may find that the top of a Needle (though
as to the sense very *sharp*) appears a *broad, blunt*, and
very *irregular* end; not resembling a Cone, as is imagined,
but only a piece of tapering body, with a great part of the
top removed, or deficient. The Points of Pins are yet more
blunt, and the Points of the most curious Mathematical
Instruments do very seldom arrive at so great a sharpness;
how much therefore can be built upon demonstrations made
only by the productions of the Ruler and Compasses, he will
be better able to consider that shall but view those *points* and
lines with a *Microscope*.

Now though this point be commonly accounted the sharp-
est (whence when we would express the sharpness of a point
the most *superlatively*, we say, As sharp as a Needle) yet the
Microscope can afford us hundreds of Instances of Points
many thousand times sharper: such as those of the *hairs*,
and *bristles*, and *claws* of multitudes of *Insects*; the *thorns*,
or *crooks*, or *hairs* of *leaves*, and other small vegetables; nay,
the ends of the *stiriæ* or small *parallelipipeds* of *Amianthus*,
and *alumen plumosum*; of many of which, though the
Points are so sharp as not to be visible, though viewed with
a *Microscope* (which magnifies the Object, in bulk, above a
million of times) yet I doubt not, but were we able *practically*
to make *Microscopes* according to the *theory* of them, we
might find hills, and dales, and pores, and sufficient breadth,
or expansion, to give all those parts elbow-room, even in the

blunt top of the very Point of any of these so very sharp bodies. For certainly the *quantity* or extension of any body may be *Divisible in infinitum*, though perhaps not the *matter*.

But to proceed: The point of a small and very sharp Needle nevertheless appeared through the *Microscope* above a quarter of an inch broad, not round nor flat, but *irregular*, and *uneven*; so that it seemed to have been big enough to have afforded a hundred armed Mites room enough to be ranged by each other without endangering the breaking of one another's necks, by being thrust off on either side. The surface of which, though appearing to the naked eye very smooth, could not nevertheless hide a multitude of holes and scratches and ruggednesses from being discovered by the Microscope to invest it, several of which inequalities (seeming like *holes* made by some small specks of *Rust*; or some *adventitious* body that stuck very close to it) were *casual*. All the rest that roughen the surface were only so many marks of the rudeness and bungling of *Art*. So inaccurate is it, in all its productions, even in those which seem most neat, that if examined with an organ more acute than that by which they were made, the more we see of their *shape*, the less appearance will there be of their *beauty*: whereas in the works of *Nature*, the deepest Discoveries show us the greatest Excellencies. An evident Argument, that he that was the Author of all these things, was no other than *Omnipotent*; being able to include as great a variety of parts and contrivances in the yet smallest Discernible Point, as in those vaster bodies (which comparatively are called also Points) such as the *Earth, Sun,* or *Planets*. Nor need it seem strange that the Earth itself may be by an Analogy called a Physical Point: For as its body, though now so near us as to fill our eyes and fancies with a sense of the vastness of it, may by a little Distance, and some convenient Diminishing Glasses, be made to vanish into a scarce visible Speck, or Point (as I have often tried on the *Moon*, and (when not too bright) on the Sun itself.) So, could a Mechanical contrivance successfully answer our *Theory*, we might see the least spot as big as the Earth itself; and Discover, as Descartes also conjectures, as great a variety of bodies in the *Moon*, or *Planets*, as in the *Earth*.

Adapted for Reliquiae by the editors

Judi Sutherland
Following Teisa (Excerpt)

Tees Head to Cow Green

How it wells up from nowhere to chase
gravity downhill, becomes a rill,
a rickle of old stones, then hurtles rocks,
purls and pools in reeds, broadens, welcomes in
the tribute of the lesser streams, sways,
nudging its banks, goes garlanded with bridges,
then, brackish in the estuary's slow tide,
pours itself to sea, oblivious.
Where does the river begin?
With the first drop falling from a blade of grass,
among the tussocks, haggs and groughs,
a peaty trickle soaking through the moor. Headwaters
where snow makes landfall on Cross Fell's eastern slope,
high on the spine of England. My grandmother would say,
count the weather over from America; five days from New York
it reaches here, rolling a New World of cloud picked up
on its Atlantic passage. Here is where it disembarks.
This river has a northern voice, sampling the geology
with a liquid tongue, the southernmost of three,
hauling Pennine waters to the great North Sea.
It channels the steady rain that rinses out the heather,
carrying the stain of iron and bitumen
and the deaths of flowers, down from the watershed,
tasting the rain and the meltwaters. Tees flows faster
than any other, roiling, bubbling, waterfalling;
two days ride down to South Gare breakwater.
Kittling over dolerite, the new river goes paddling,

telling tales of moss and all the secrets buried
in the peat. Gathering Trout Beck from Great Dun Fell —
where water pounding down the leat
washes out lead-laden ore in hushing-gulleys.
It finds a lake submerged within a lake,
the old Weel, swollen and penned back
for the factories, ninety miles downstream,
that used to thirst and beg for water.
Red grouse low-fly in pairs, skimming over heather;
a curlew calls, the sheep bleat back an answer.
Under the wavelets, a bronze age village drowses
drowned; sleeptalking of the ancient days
when Cow Green pastured cows
and was green.

Roz Quillan Chandler
the past is

...now I've learnt your secret names I'll have to leave – I've
     wrestled against winter
mist and rain, heard silence ricochet in the wind, seen the last
     of last year's leaves
scatter and disappear, lost my way trespassing through
     neglected valley woods –
had time to listen to owls whisper meaning into the night,
     cheered the first three
early swallows coming fast from the south, day after day kept a
     close eye on the
intentions of wren blackbird goldfinch, every morning hailed
     wild geese skeining
noisily past, caught glimpses of stoats out to kill, raptors
     harassing doves, followed
all manner of good bad hasty dash, quick hesitation along
     hawthorn hedges and
grassy banks – watched slow bumblebee foragers steadily work
     opening flowers –
I've accepted the challenge of dusk, leapt boulders, hop-
     scotched rocky paths down
from The Beacon, trembled at the speed, raced along the
     mossy stone-walled

Lower Grumbla road, hurrying home through the last of the
    light, frightening
myself with myths and haunted oaks — counted loneliness as a
    gift, apart from the
blue depths of one starry night — I've walked beside cold clear
    running water,
looked into moorland quarries and considered — taken one
    terrible footstep after
another across burnt bracken acres, grieved for the
    inescapable raw red terror, for
fire-scorched lives — I've made pilgrimage, wished at your
    sacred well, sat for hours
in the granite-circled churchyard finding some kind of quiet in
    the solitude, felt
kinship across thousands of years with hut dwellers
    swineherds priests servants
congregations farmers lovers artists and wayfarers all. Soon I'll
    have to leave. I
knew from the beginning there'd be a time I could no longer
    stop stand and stare —
I'll leave, when the valley's green and the cuckoo arrives...

ta-poŋ'-hu

the cheek-bone

śuŋk-ćiŋ'ća

a young wolf

wa-kiŋ'-yaŋ

to fly, a great bird, thunder

wa-na'-ġi-ya-ta

in the world of spirits

C.S. Mills
A visitor at the end of winter

She arrives, without fail, when the first green shoots emerge
through the snow. But her arrival is no surprise; we've seen
the signs, paradoxical as they may be, for some weeks. And
we recount them for her:

White shoulder of deep snow turning
Something rising steadily in the veils of flame
Black water through thick ice

She arrives, folds her wings, and sits quietly beside the
hearth, tracing designs in the ashes with her toe. She doesn't
demand praise, but still:

You many-dimensional rise, gentle knoll
You bath of milk, unmoved multiplier
Here a brilliant three-faced goddess

She leaves at sunset and we rush to the hearth to look at the
designs. They make little sense, but we interpret them as
best we can. Join us, if you like:

Circle sunwise, place a coin in the spring
Cut the reeds, weave them into four spokes
Take some water and sprinkle it round the belly

Janil Uc Tun
Colección de insectos que volaron sobre mi cabeza /
Collection of Insects that Flew Around My Head (Excerpts)

A Minerva Tun

I

Me deshebré del vestido azul de mi madre
caí al suelo
como solo suelen caerse algunas piedras
de barrancos altos
de precipitadas aguas pluviales
del exacto polvo de algunas alas trasparentes.

Me abandoné a una esquina de periódicos viejos
que contaban historias inconclusas
de fantasmas errantes en las carreteras.

Me agrieté como la madera rancia de los armarios
como el fuego que sublima la hoja
como todos los nombres que he tenido:
termita, hormiga, polilla.
Mi madre es una fotografía devorada por insectos.

For Minerva Tun

I

I got rid of my mother's blue dress
and fell to the floor
like stones from a high ravine
falling because of precipitous
rainwater from
the exact dust of some transparent wings.

I abandoned myself to a corner of old newspapers
that told unfinished stories
of ghosts wandering the roads.

I cracked like the musty wood of the wardrobe
like the fire that sublimates the leaf
like all the names that I have had:
termite, ant, moth.
My mother is a photograph devoured by insects.

II

Insectos comen el vestido azul de mi madre,
pero no se detienen ahí,
comen todo lo que ha tocado:
el neceser con arreglo de flores amarillas
el reloj de tres agujas
mi columpio bajo la sombra del cedro
la abarquillada mesa de planchado
y la lámina gris de la cocina
que se menea en los días de lluvia.

A veces me subo a su bicicleta
encadenada al zaguán de la casa
hago girar sus ruedas en círculos de caucho
e imagino que soy mi madre
manejando en pasadizos subterráneos
a la ciudad donde habitan los pájaros negros.

A la abuela se le ha hecho tarde
el cielo parpadea la noche:
hoy no me llevará a ver las mariposas
que vuelan sobre el camino blanco.

II

Insects eat my mother's blue dress,
but they don't stop there,
they eat everything they touch:
the bag with an arrangement of yellow flowers
the watch with three hands
my swing under the shade of the cedar
the curled up ironing board
and the gray kitchen laminate
that ripples on rainy days.

Sometimes I get on my bike
chained in the front hall of my house
I spin the wheels in rubber circles
and I imagine that I am my mother
driving in underground passage ways
to the city where the black birds live.

Grandmother has been late
the sky flashes the night:
today she won't take me to see the butterflies
that fly over the white path.

VIII

Naufragan pájaros negros en mi ventana
huyen de una lechuza que desparrama su canto
sobre mi alto cedro.

Mi abuela sale en las noches
a hacer ruidos con trastes y cucharas
a tirar piedras a los árboles
a maldecir en lenguas que no entiendo.

Yo me quedo en casa
y convierto los frutos del cedro
en venados que cazan jaguares
y en guacamayas que nadan con los peces.

cont.

VIII

Shipwrecked blackbirds on my window
flee an owl that scatters its song
on my tall cedar.

My grandmother goes out at night
making noises with dishes and spoons
throwing stones at the trees
cursing in languages I don't understand.

I stay inside
and turn the fruits of the cedar
into deer that hunt jaguars
into macaws that swim with fish.

Cuando mi abuela vuelve
aplasta la casa de mis animales
como una zarigüeya gigante de dientes afilados
y me dice que esta noche dormiré con ella
porque pronto vendrá la lluvia de la ceniza
y debo aprender a moler el maíz que siembro
porque no todos los pájaros mueren volando.

Hoy cayó granizo
y la abuela no me dejó jugar con el hielo.

Lechuza del tiempo:
vuela lejos de nosotras
vete para el norte,
a ese lugar donde perdimos a mi madre.

When my grandmother comes back in
she smashes the animals' house
like a giant opossum with sharp teeth
and tells me that tonight I will sleep with her
because soon the rain of ash will come
and I should learn to grind the corn that I plant
because not all birds die flying.

Hail fell today
and grandmother wouldn't let me play with the ice.

Owl of time:
fly far from us
head north,
to the place where we lost my mother.

IX

Madre,
llévate mi colección de insectos
mis alas de mariposas
los ojos de mis libélulas
mis luciérnagas apagadas:
todos mis frascos de escarabajos
y las historias que me contaron.

Madre,
cuando vuelvas me llevarás al camino blanco
a recoger todos los cadáveres de insectos
a ponerles nombres
a contarles historias.

Madre,
la abuela dice que el desierto
son cientos de hebras que no forman tejido
y que las mujeres que saben tejer
no pueden perderse.

cont.

IX

Mother,
take my collection of insects
my butterfly wings
the eyes of the dragon flies
my extinguished fireflies:
all my jars of beetles
and the stories they told me.

Mother,
when you return you'll take me to the white road
to collect all the bodies of insects
to give them names
to tell them stories.

Mother,
grandmother says in the desert
there are hundreds of threads that do not form a fabric
and that the women who know how to knit
cannot get lost.

Madre,
cuando debas irte
lleva mi botella blanca para cargar agua
mi sábana de animalitos verde,
mi columpio debajo del cedro
lleva el cesto de caimitos de la abuela
y escupe las semillas en el camino.

Madre,
sé que lo pájaros dejan sus plumas cuando llueve
no tienes que decírmelo.
Se hace tarde,
vete antes de que las cigarras despierten
antes que las luciérnagas se posen en los ojos de la abuela.

Mother,
when you leave
take my white bottle to carry water
my green bed sheet of little animals,
my swing under the cedar
take grandmother's basket of star apples
and spit out the seeds along the way.

Mother,
I know the birds lose their feathers when it rains
you don't have to tell me
go before the cicadas wake up
before the fireflies land on grandmother's eyes.

X

Abuela,
en la escuela aprendí que las mariposas monarcas
son insectos migrantes
quienes terminan sus viajes son sus hijas y sus nietas.

Abuela,
no le creas a los periódicos
no le creas a los disfraces de la gente
ellos no conocen a mi madre
creen que ella es un número o un apodo
que es otra que se perdió yendo hacia el norte.

Abuela,
entona desde tu hamaca tus canciones desafinadas
calienta el agua del pozo para que beba
sacude las polillas que anidan en tu cabeza.

cont.

X

Grandmother,
in school I learned that monarch butterflies
are migratory insects
and the ones who finish the journey are their daughters and
granddaughters.

Grandmother,
don't believe the newspapers
don't believe the disguises of the people
they don't know my mother
they think she's just a number or a name
just another one who got lost going north.

Grandmother,
sing your off-tune songs from your hammock
heat the water from the well to drink
shake off the moths that nest in your head.

Abuela,
continuarán las lluvias en el otoño
y el viejo cedro caerá sobre la casa
derramará un bosque en tu boca abierta
para que les chifles a los grillos.

Abuela,
no han llegado cartas de mi madre
ya no veo sus fotos por ningún lado
recuerda que dijiste que cuando me ponga su vestido azul
me subirás al columpio debajo del cedro
y cuando despierte estaremos en el norte.

El calendario da vueltas sobre sí mismo:
ya migraron todos los pájaros.
Las mariposas no vuelan mientras duermen.

Grandmother,
the rains will continue into autumn
and the old cedar will fall on the house
spill a forest in your open mouth
so that you wheeze with the crickets.

Grandmother,
no letters from my mother have arrived
I don't see her photos anywhere
remember you said when I put on the blue dress
you would lift me up on the swing under the cedar
and when I woke up we'd be in the north.

The calendar revolves on itself:
all the birds have migrated.
Butterflies do not fly when they are sleeping.

XI

Duermen escarabajos verdes
en la panza del cedro
también hay termitas y hormigas rojas,
es una gala de insectos el gran féretro
que no sobrevivió al otoño.

La abuela mece su hamaca
mientras varios hombres cortan mi árbol
es buena leña, dice la abuela
y yo lloro como si fuera mi panza
la que se astilla en diminutos fragmentos.

No le hablo a la abuela en días enteros
no como su comida
no tibio su agua
no peino sus largas canas
hasta que regreso de la escuela
con los ojos cargados de nubes
y le muestro el periódico
donde dice que muchas mariposas monarcas
se pierden por la tala de sus bosques.

cont.

XI

Green beetles sleep
in the belly of the cedar
there are also termites and red ants,
it's a gala of insects the great coffin
that didn't survive autumn.

Grandmother rocks in her hammock
while several men cut my tree
it's good firewood, says grandmother
and I cry is if it were my belly
that splinters into tiny fragments.

I don't speak to grandmother for days
don't eat her food
don't heat her water
don't comb her long gray hair
until I come home from school
with my eyes full of clouds
and I show her the newspaper
where it says monarch butterflies
get lost because their forests have been cut down.

La abuela me abraza entre el humo de su cigarro
y me dice que mañana sembraremos otro cedro
donde broten todos mis insectos.

Madre,
regresa con mi colección de mariposas,
te la presté para que regreses
Madre, la casa se deshebra en girones de tiempo.

My grandmother hugs me along with the smoke of her cigar
and tells me that tomorrow we will plant another cedar
where all my insects sprout.

Mother,
come back with my collection of butterflies,
I lent them to you so you would return
Mother, the house is torn apart in shreds of time.

Translated from Spanish
by Don Cellini

Christine Morro
haunt

Old Norse *heimta*
to lead home

in the shifting light of late afternoon
a finger traces a single line

an invitation across mineral dark waters

its wind-thrummed surface becomes
a shoaling of iridescent fish

flowing out of the present
into where our ancestors dwell

before moonrise
our eyes adjust to the evenfall

we are called to dance
release

we merge with each mellow slap
of wave meeting shore

~

here i learn
water presses light
light presses mineral, quartz, schist

a postscript to the main poem, river

traces of a thousand mornings
ochre, copper, meadow-brown

a marbling of silt held in geologic time

silence is devotion

Alba — dawn
the flexion of water

i am held by wilderness

a-i'-de-ṡa-ṡa-

in the red flame

kiŋ-yaŋ'-pi

those that fly, birds

ka-ḣmiŋ

a bend in a river

wa-kiŋ'-yaŋ-ho-toŋ

the thunder utters his voice

Thomas Browne
Urn Burial (Excerpts)

Time hath endlesse rarities, and shows of all varieties; which reveals old things in heaven, makes new discoveries in earth, and even earth itself a discovery.

*

Many have taken voluminous pains to determine the state of the soul upon disunion; but men have been most phantasticall in the singular contrivances of their corporall dissolution: whilst the sobrest Nations have rested in two wayes, of simple inhumation and burning.

*

Urnall interments and burnt Reliques lye not in fear of
worms, or to be an heritage for Serpents; In carnall sepul-
ture, corruptions seem peculiar unto parts, and some speak
of snakes out of the spinal marrow.

*

Before *Plato* could speak, the soul had wings in *Homer*,
which fell not, but flew out of the body into the mansions of
the dead.

*

But the secret and symbolicall hint was the harmonical
nature of the soul; which delivered from the body, went
again to enjoy the primitive harmony of heaven, from
whence it first descended; which according to its progresse
traced by antiquity, came down by *Cancer*, and ascended by
Capricornus.

*

That they powred oyle upon the pyre, was a tolerable prac-
tise, while the intention rested in facilitating the ascension;
But to place good *Omens* in the quick and speedy burning, to
sacrifice unto windes for a dispatch in this office, was a low
form of superstition.

*

Our dayes become considerable like petty sums by minute
accumulations; where numerous fractions make up but small
round numbers; and our dayes of a span long make not one
little finger.

*

Life is a pure flame, and we live by an invisible Sun within
us.

Richard Skelton
The Body from Scaleby Moss

25 May 1834

who is she
this residual this relique
her skin daubed a river's colour
her mind sieved and cased in the hide of a deer

remnants hand the bog tympanic
remnants hand the almost neck
the spine body
we now carry the corrupted word

and the soft putty of mosses
absent membranes
calcium throats
eye pouches

(peat formed from decaying plants
combined with humic and fulvic acids
and the residues of insects algae fungi)

insects
the pupal earth the soil her chrysalis
the cloak she gathered about herself
her pharate body

we have brought her out too early
too late to reinter her
to close the wound

the earth an instant for this leather bone woman
long in her dwelling her stained orbits
they called it birth they called it *the living after living*

anterior of the coronal country
mineral light
brain flora
daughter isotopes

and even the sun cannot explain
her unlit chambers of vision

Walter K. Kelly
On Sacred Trees

The primeval drink of immortality is called *soma* by the
Hindus and *haoma* by the Zend branch of the Aryans.[1]
These names are identical; the plants which yield the juices
so called are different, but resemble each other in both hav-
ing knotty stems. The haoma plant grows like the vine, but
its leaves are like those of the jessamine; the Indian soma
is now extracted from the *Asclepias acida*.[2] The Iranians, or
West Aryans, describe two kinds of haoma, the white and
the yellow. The former is a fabulous plant, believed to be the
same as the gaokerena of the Zendavesta; the latter, which
is used in religious rites, and is extolled for its yellow colour,
as soma is in India, grows on mountains, and was known
to Plutarch. The Parsees of India send one of their priests
from time to time to Kirmân to procure supplies of the plant
for sacred uses. The fabulous white haoma, or *gaokerena*,
grows in heaven, near another tree called the 'impassive' or
'inviolable', which bears the seeds of every kind of vegetable

life. Both grow in the Vouru Kasha lake, in which ten fish keep incessant watch upon a lizard, sent by the evil power Agramainyus (Ahriman) for the destruction of the haoma. The 'inviolable' tree is called also the eagle's, or, according to some, the owl's tree. A bird of one kind or the other, but most probably an eagle, sits on its top. When he rises from it, a thousand branches shoot forth; when he perches again, he breaks a thousand branches and makes their seed fall. Another bird, that is constantly beside him, picks them up, and carries them to where Tistar draws water, which he then rains down upon the earth with the seeds it contains. The two trees — the eagle's and the white haoma — appear to have been originally one. The hostile lizard is the serpent or dragon of India, already known to us as the ravisher of the Âpas, and the harvest-spoiler.

Besides the earthly soma the Hindus recognise a heavenly soma or *amrita* (ambrosia) that drops from the imperishable *asvattha* or *peepul* (*Ficus religiosa*), out of which the immortals shaped the heavens and the earth. Beneath this mighty tree, which spreads its branches over the third heaven, dwell Yama and the Pitris, and quaff the drink of immortality with the gods. At its foot grow plants of all healing virtue, incorporations of the soma. Two birds sit on its top, one of them eating figs, whilst the other looks on without eating, and others again press out the soma juice from its branches. These details are from the Vedas; later writings have preserved the ancient tradition that the soma-dropping tree bears fruit and seed of every kind in the world. They call the tree Ilpa, and say it grows in Brahma's world, surrounded by lake Âra, beyond the ageless stream, which renews the youth of those who but behold it, or at least of those who bathe in it.

The parallelism between the Indian and the Iranian world-tree on the one hand, and the Ash Yggdrasil on the other, is very striking. The latter extends its branches over the whole world, and they reach higher than heaven; beneath them the gods have their chief and holiest abode. The tree has three roots, one striking upwards to heaven, one towards the home of the frost giants, and one towards the under-world. From beneath each root springs a sacred fountain, the Urdhrbrunnr, the Mimirbrunnr, and the Hvergelmir. The first has its name from Urdhr, the Norn or Fate, and beside it the gods and the Norns had their judgment-seat. Every morn-ing the Norns draw water from their fountain and pour it on the branches of the ash; it falls from them into the valleys as honey-dew, and the bees feed upon it. The precious water in the second fountain — Mimir's — is so charged with wisdom and understanding, that only for one draught of it Odin pledged his eye, and laid it as a pawn in the well. An eagle sits on the tree, and a hawk between the eagle's eyes. Four stags roam about the forest-like ash. Through the branches and the roots creep many serpents, chief among which is Nidhöggr. That deadly serpent or dragon lies in Hvergelmir, the infernal fountain, and gnaws at the roots; whilst the squirrel Ratatöskr runs up and down, and tries to stir up strife between Nidhöggr and the eagle. The water of Mimir's well is mead, that of the Urdhrbrunnr falls as honey-dew from the ash; honey is the chief ingredient in mead, and a main one in soma. Soma, mead, and honey are mythically one; and each and all of them are identical with the precious rain that drops from the cloud-tree, and fills the fountains or lakes in which its roots are dipped.

Yggdrasil, this cloud-tree of the Norseman, was an ash (Norse, *askr*), the tree out of which the gods formed the first man, who was thence called Askr. The ash was also among the Greeks an image of the clouds, and the mother of men.

Phoroneus, in whom in the Peloponnesian legend recognised the fire-bringer and the first man, was the son of the river-god Inachos and the nymph Melia, i.e., the ash.

There were many Grecian nymphs of this name, and all of
them were daughters either of Oceanos or of Poseidon, sea-
gods whose domain was originally the cloud-sea, and whose
daughters, one and all, were originally cloud-goddesses. One
of these Melian nymphs was carried off by the summer-god
Apollo, who killed her brother Kaanthos with his arrows,
when the latter, failing to recover his sister, set fire to the
sacred grove of the ravisher. The tomb of Kaanthos was to
be seen near the fountain of Ismenios, sacred to Ares, who
placed a dragon there to keep guard over it. Now, Kaanthos,
or, with the digamma restored, Kavanthos, answers exactly
to the Sanscrit Kavandha or Kabandha, which means a
big-bellied cask, a cloud of that form, or a demon dwelling
in such a cloud. In the Greek legend this demon flings fire
(lightning) at his sister's ravisher, who kills him as Indra
killed Kabandha. The fountain sacred to Ares, a god of
winter and the under-world, and the dragon that guards it,
is Hvergelmir, the infernal fountain at the foot of Yggdrasil,
with its inmate, the dragon Nidhöggr; and, to complete
the parallel, we have but to replace the Ismenian fountain
at the foot of the ash (Melia), where doubtless it lay orig-
inally, before the myth had been localised as a legendary
tale. A third Melia is the mother of Amykos by Poseidon
Genethlios, whose surname marks him emphatically as the
god at whose disposal is the moisture that is the cause of
all fruitfulness and nourishment. His connection therefore
with Melia distinctly represents the Aryan tree, in which are
comprised the seeds of all vegetation. A fourth Melia is the
daughter of Poseidon and wife of Danaos, a husband and a
father that show what was her own nature, for the watering
of the arid Argos was ascribed, as a most remarkable feat, to
Danaos and his daughter. Lastly, there is a Melia who bears
to Silenos a son Pholos, who is one of the Centaurs, a race of
cloud-demons.

Another indication of the original cloud-nature of these Melian or ash nymphs is seen in the fact that the Dodonæan legends put in place of them, as nurses of Zeus, the Hyades, the nymphs of the constellation that rises at the rainy and stormy season of the year. Furthermore, there is a fragment of the poetess Moiro, preserved by Athenæus, which describes the infant Zeus as being fed in Crete with nectar brought by the eagle; so that whilst the Meliai or nymphs of the ash appear as personifications of an older Grecian world-tree, this story of the eagle shows that the birds who also lodged in the tree were once known to the Greeks.

Phoroneus was not the only man known in Greek story who was born of the ash. According to Hesiod, Jove made the third or brazen race out of ash-trees; but the same idea must have been entertained in a still more comprehensive form, for another authority states that the *first* race of men sprang from the Melian nymphs; and Hesychius says in direct terms, 'The fruit of the ash: the race of men.'

We have not yet exhausted the list of analogies between Yggdrasil and the Grecian ash, for the latter was, like the former, a honey-dropping tree. Its name implies no less, for *melia*, ash, and *meli*, *melit*, honey, have the same root, *mel*, which is found in many other words with the sense of sweet, pleasing, delightful. There was a positive, as well as a mythic, reason why the Greeks should give the ash a name signifying sweetness, because the *Fraxinus ornus*, a species of ash indigenous in the south of Europe, yields *manna* from its slit bark. They may also have conceived that honey dropped upon the earth as dew from the heavenly ash, for Theophrastus mentions a kind of honey which fell in that form from the air, and which was therefore called *aeromeli*. We now perceive the reason why the honey-giving nymphs of the ash and the honey-giving bees (*melissai*) were so assimilated in the minds of the Greeks, that the nurses of the infant Zeus (Meliai) were called by them indifferently Meliai and Melissai. The goat Amaltheia gave him her milk, and the nymphs, his nurses, fed him with their golden produce. Among the ancient Germans that sacred food was the first that was put to the lips of the newborn babe. So it was also among the Hindus, as appears from a passage in one of their sacred books: 'The father puts his mouth to the right ear of the newborn babe, and murmurs three times, "Speech! Speech!" Then he gives it a name, "Thou art Veda"; that is its secret name. Then he mixes clotted milk, honey, and butter, and feeds the babe with it out of pure gold.' The superstitious reverence in which bees are everywhere held makes it probable that a similar practice prevailed among all Indo-European races. It is found in a very surprising shape among one Celtic people:

'Lightfoot says that in the Highlands of Scotland, at the birth of an infant, the nurse takes a green stick of ash, one end of which she puts into the fire, and while it is burning, receives in a spoon the sap that oozes from the other, which she administers to the child as its first food.'

Amazing toughness of popular tradition! Some thousands of years ago the ancestors of this Highland nurse had known the *Fraxinus ornus* in Arya, or on their long journey thence through Persia, Asia Minor, and the South of Europe, and they had given its honey-like juice, as divine food, to their children; and now their descendant, imitating their practice in the cold North, but totally ignorant of its true meaning, puts the nauseous sap of her native ash into the mouth of her hapless charge, because her mother and her grandmother, and her grandmother's grandmother had done the same thing before her.

'The reason', we are told by a modern native authority, 'for giving ash-sap to newborn children in the Highlands of Scotland, is, first, because it acts as a powerful astringent;

and, secondly, because the ash, in common with the rowan, is supposed to possess the property of resisting the attacks of witches, fairies, and other imps of darkness. Without some precaution of this kind they would *change* the child, or possibly steal it away altogether. The herd boys in the district of Buchan, in Aberdeenshire, always prefer a herding stick of ash to any other wood, for in throwing at their cattle it is *sure* not to strike on a vital part, and so kill or injure the animal as a stick of any other kind of wood might do:

> Rowan, ash, and red thread
> Keep the devils frae their speed.

'It is a common practice with the housewives in the same district to tie a piece of red worsted thread round their cows' tails previous to turning them out to grass for the first time in the spring. It secures their cattle, they say, from an evil eye, from being elfshot by fairies,' &c.

The sap of the ash, tapped on certain days in spring, is drank in Germany as a remedy for the bites of serpents; and the Czecks in Bohemia eat honey (of which ash-sap is the equivalent) fasting, on Holy Thursday, thinking that it will protect them throughout the year against the usual effects of such accidents, as well as against poisons in general. They also give their cattle pieces of bread and honey for the same purpose, and throw some before sunrise into the wells and fountains, in order that the water may remain pure and clear, and free from frogs and other vermin. In Cornwall, venomous reptiles are never known to rest under the shadow of an ash, and a single blow from an ash stick is instant death to an adder. Struck by a bough of any other tree, the reptile is said to retain marks of life until the sun goes down.

According to Pliny, a serpent will rather leap into fire than into the shadow of an ash-tree. When it is touched with an ash rod, it lies as if dead; and out of a circle drawn round it while it sleeps, with such an instrument, the creature cannot escape. This inherent virtue of the ash was known also to the Greeks, as appears from a fragment of Nicander. A contributor to Wolf's *Journal* states that the wood of the tree, cut at certain holy seasons, is reputed to be incorruptible and to heal wounds – a property due, no doubt, to the amrita with which it is impregnated. Its character as an embodiment of fire, of which we have already had so many evidences, is manifested in a remarkable Swedish legend, quoted by Grimm, which tells that some seafaring people received an ash-tree from a blind giant, with instructions to set it upon the altar of a church he wished to destroy. Instead of doing as he bade them, they placed the ash on the mound over a grave, which instantly burst into bright flames. The grave it may be presumed, was that of an unholy being of the old pagan times. Plot says in his *History of Staffordshire,* 'The common people believe, that 'tis very dangerous to break a bough from the ash, to this very day.' The sacredness of the tree is further shown by the fact, recently discovered, that courts were held under it at Froidnow in Schweiz, and Buochs in Unterwalden. Grimm has expressed his surprise at nowhere finding any traces of a practice which seemed likely to have been universal among the Germans, since the gods sat in judgment under the ash Yggdrasil. The supposition that the hazel, which stands in close mythical relationship to the ash, almost entirely supplanted the latter in judicial usages, affords a probable explanation of the anomaly.

There are facts tending strongly to the conclusion, though they may not suffice to place it beyond all question, that a world-wide tree, with its appurtenances, was a conception known to the Romans in early times. All the qualities belonging to a bird connected with such a tree are exhibited, explicitly or by implication, in the history of their Picus; and

the descent of men from trees appears to have been a popu-
lar belief in Italy as well as in Greece.

> Hæc nemora indigenæ Fauni Nymphæque tenebant
> Gensque virum truncis et duro robore nata.
>
> Æn. VIII., 314

> These woods were first the seat of sylvan powers,
> Of nymphs and fauns, and savage men, who took
> Their birth from trunks of trees and stubborn oak.
>
> Dryden

> Quippe aliter tunc orbe novo cœloque recenti
> Vivebant homines, qui rupto robore nati,
> Compositive luto, nullos habuere parentes.
>
> Juvenal, Sat. VI., 11.

> For when the world was new, the race that broke,
> Unfathered, from the soil or opening oak.
> Lived most unlike the men of later times.
>
> Gifford

In another passage Virgil speaks of a sacred tree, the
œsculus, in a manner which Grimm has noticed as strikingly
suggestive of Yggdrasil:

> Æsculus in primis, quæ quantum vortice ad auras
> Ætherias, tantum radice in tartara tendit.
>
> Georg. II., 291

> Jove's own tree,
> High as his topmost boughs to heaven ascend,
> So low his roots to hell's dominions tend.
>
> Dryden

Evidently these lines have a mythical import. The æsculus was a species of oak sacred to Jove; and in Greece the oak, as well as the ash, was accounted a tree from which men had sprung. The disguised hero of the Odyssey is asked to state his pedigree, since he must needs have one, 'for', says the interrogator, 'belike you are not come of the oak told of in old times, nor of the rock'. The 'ruminal fig-tree' seems to play a part in the legend of the foundation of Rome like that attributed to the oak by the Greeks and to the ash by the Germans. Picus also has his share in the legend, for he helped the she-wolf to nourish the twins; and though Ovid does not tell us what kind of ailment he gave them, we may venture to surmise that he fed them with the mead which he himself loved so well, in like manner as the eagle in Crete fed the infant Jove with nectar, the equivalent of mead.

The mythic characteristics of the ash help to explain some English superstitions, the true meaning of which appears to have been generally misunderstood. White says in his *Natural History of Selborne*, 'At the south corner of the area near the church there stood about twenty years ago a very old grotesque hollow pollard ash, which for ages had been looked on with no small veneration as a shrew-ash. Now a shrew-ash is an ash whose twigs or branches, when gently applied to the limbs of cattle, will immediately relieve the pains which a beast suffers from the running of a shrew-mouse over the part affected. For it is supposed that a shrew-mouse is of so baneful and deleterious a nature, that wherever it creeps over a beast, be it horse, cow, or sheep, the suffering animal is afflicted with cruel anguish, and threatened with the loss of the use of the limb. Against this accident, to which they were continually liable, our provident forefathers always kept a shrew-ash at hand, which, when once medicated, would maintain its virtue for ever. A shrew-ash was made thus: Into the body a deep hole was bored with an auger, and a poor devoted shrew-mouse was thrust in alive, and plugged in, no doubt with several quaint incantations long since forgotten. As the ceremonies necessary for such a consecration are no longer understood, all succession is at an end, and no such tree is known to subsist in the manor or hundred. As to that on the area, "the late vicar stubbed and burned it", when he was waywarden, regardless of the remonstrances of the bystanders, who interceded in vain for its preservation.'

It is manifest that this practice was founded principally upon the supposed virtue inherent in the ash of neutralising every kind of venom. It is a tree that will tolerate nothing poisonous within its shadow, and wounds are cured with its sap. As to the intersection of the shrew-mouse within it, this may very probably have been done in accordance with a medical doctrine of great antiquity – the doctrine of sympathy. The spear of Achilles healed with one end of its ashen shaft the wound it had made with the other; it was a common practice, so common as to have given rise to a well-known proverb, to mix some hairs of a dog with the salve laid on the part he had bitten; and there have been famous leeches who cured sword wounds by applying their remedies, not to the patient, but to the weapon. 'Fairies', says Grose, 'sometimes shoot at cattle with arrows headed with flint stones; these are often found and are called elfshots. In order to effect the cure of an animal so injured, it is to be touched with one of those elfshots, or to be made drink the water in which one has been dipped.' The venom of the shrew-mouse, neutralised by the sap of the ash, would co-operate with it in curing the injured limb to which the twigs were applied. A correspondent sent the following scrap from a newspaper to *Notes and Queries*, vol v., p. 581: 'At Oldham, last week, a woman summoned the owner of a dog that had bitten her. She said she should not have adopted this course had the owner of

the animal given her some of its hair, to ensure her against
any evil consequences from the bite.'

There stood in the village of Selborne in Gilbert White's
time 'a row of pollard ashes, which,' he says, 'by the seams
and long cicatrices down their sides, manifestly show that
in former times they have been cleft asunder. These trees,
when young and flexible, were severed and held open by
wedges, while ruptured children, stripped naked, were
pushed through the apertures, under a persuasion that
by such a process the poor babies would be cured of their
infirmity. As soon as the operation was over, the tree, in the
suffering part, was plastered with loam and carefully swathed
up. If the part coalesced and soldered together, as usually fell
out where the feat was performed with any adroitness at all,
the party was cured; but where the cleft continued to gape,
the operation, it was supposed, would prove ineffectual. We
have several persons now living in the village, who in their
childhood were supposed to be healed by this superstitious
ceremony, derived down perhaps from our Saxon ancestors,
who practised it before their conversion to Christianity.'

This mode of cure has not yet gone quite out of use
in England, so far as the ash is concerned, and it is still
a practice much in vogue in the southern counties, when
children are suffering from whooping-cough and some other
complaints, to make them pass through the loop formed by a
bramble which has taken root at both ends. This custom, and
that of passing children and cattle through perforated earth
or rocks, or through natural or artificial openings in trees,
especially the ash and the oak, is common to most European
countries. There was a bushy oak near Wittstock in Altmark,
the branches of which had grown together again at some
distance from the stem, leaving open spaces between them.
Whoever crept through these spaces was freed from his
malady, whatever it might be, and many crutches lay about,

which had been thrown away by visitors to the tree who no longer needed them. Close to the road passing through the forest of Süllingswald, there was an aged oak with a hole shaped like the eye of a needle in its huge stem. This gave the foresters and charcoal burners a welcome opportunity for 'hanselling' strangers who passed that way, that is to say, forcing them to pay a small sum if they did not wish to be dragged through the needle's eye. This custom of hanselling travellers kept its ground after the belief in the healing virtue of the tree had died out.

'This creeping through oak-cleft, earth or stone,' says Grimm, 'seems a transference of the malady or the bewitchment to the genius of the tree or the earth.' But this is not a satisfactory explanation; for though such a mode of shifting off bodily disorders from men to trees is well known, nothing of the kind appears to have been intended in the case in question. For the cure of hernia, for instance, it was thought essential that the cleft tree should become whole again. Moreover, Grimm's theory is manifestly untenable with reference to a cure-working hole in a church wall, such as that of Stappenbeck, to which 'there was formerly a great resort of sick people, for whenever one of them crept through it he was instantly cured. But it lost its virtue at last when sick animals were made to pass through it, and then it was stopped up.' The best explanation which has been given of this superstition is that proposed by Liebrecht, who thinks that the whole proceeding was originally designed to symbolise the new birth of the patient, who, coming naked again into the world, left all his former maladies behind him. It appears indeed to be a close copy of a Hindu religious usage, and probably had its origin, like the latter, in times previous to the dispersion of the Aryans.

'For the purpose of regeneration,' says Coleman, 'it is directed to make an image of pure gold, of the female power of nature, in the shape either of a woman or of a cow. In this statue the person to be regenerated is enclosed and dragged through the usual channel. As a statue of pure gold and proper dimensions would be too expensive, it is sufficient to make an image of the sacred yoni, through which the person to be regenerated is to pass... Perforated rocks are considered as emblems of the yoni, through which pilgrims and others pass for the purpose of being regenerated. The utmost faith is placed in this sin-expelling transit.'

The Hindu custom symbolises the new birth of the soul, the European that of the body. The cloud, the matrix of the vital spark, is represented in the one by the figure of the woman or the cow, in the other by the tree, and in both by the rock.

Adapted for Reliquiae by the editors

Editors' Notes:

1　Kelly argues for an 'Ayran or Indo-European' *race* based on commonalities of language, but this is problematic because it maps racial characteristics onto linguistic and cultural phenomena. Other authors, such as de Gobineau and Chamberlain have used such arguments to bolster racist ideologies. Needless to say, Kelly, in limiting his observations to those of a shared culture, makes no such propagandist claims.

2　Now known as *Sarcostemma acidum*.

Steffi Lang
At Slaty Fork

black leaves are the only certainty, goldenrod,
the first threshold given to us
to cross. the river under
the bridge runs to wax. how an old man goes
to bury his father and finds only
the fig tree, broken.

keep in mind the auguries, three river-birds
does not mean you must drown. bees
further from nests is a winter without
blue wheat. pebble placed at the mouth and our grief
will not meet as words or moons.

/

in so far as we
diminish, so we come towards
rivers   each of us awaits that dusk
and finds only the fissure
            of presence through tree-branches

you are declined, an empty word
for landscape-presences
            hollow bough to un-echo —

fungus, ghostflower, and the book of such lichenous things
forewarns you of your wound. that these eyes, left mercurial,
would sing as stones
                and out of all the alchemies of the dark,
it is here   the river naming death and death
naming the names buried

John Gower
Confessio Amantis (Excerpt)

The God of Slepe hath made his hous,
Whiche of entaile is merveilous.
'Under an hill there is a cave
Which of the sonné may nought have,
So that no man may knowe aright
The point betwene the day and night.
There is no fire, there is no sparke,
There is no doré which may charke,
Whereof an eyé shulde unshet,
So that inwárd there is no let.
And for to speke of that withoute,
There stant no great tre night about,
Whereon there mighté crowe or pie
Alighté for to clepe or crie.
There is no cock to crowé day,
Ne besté none which noisé may
The hille, but all abouté round
There is growénd upon the ground
Poppy, which bereth the sede of slepe,
With other herbés such an hepe.

A stillé water for the nones
Rennénd upon the smallé stones,
Which hight of Lethés the rivér,
Under that hille in such manér
There is, which yiveth great appetite
To slepe. And thus ful of delite
Slepe hath his hous, and of his couche
Within his chambre if I shall touche
Of hebenus that slepy tre
The bordés all abouté be,
And for he shuldé slepé softe
Upon a fether bed alofte
He lith with many a pilwe of doun,
The chambre is strowéd up and doun
With swevenés many a thousand fold.'

Editors' Note:

    An extract from *Sloth*, Book IV of Gower's Middle English poem.

o-ka´-ḣde-će

a rent, a fracture

pe-ta´-ġa

burning coals

i-kpi´-pa-taŋ-haŋ

in around the body

na-ġi´

soul, spirit, shades, ghosts

Jasmine Gallagher
In Loving Memory Of

I   Sea Stories[1]

The mermaid of the Galway coast is like the *Marakihau* of
Māori legend – a kind of *taniwha*[2] with a human upper body
and spiral fish-like tail – which is carved on the fronts of
numerous houses in the North Island, near the Bay of Plenty.

II   Seers and Healers
      Biddy Early
      Mrs. Seridan
      Mr. Saggerton
      'A Great Warrior in the Business'
      Old Deruane

The Kākāpō (Parrot of the Night), like the mysterious Kiwi,
White Heron, Morepork, and Pekapeka (bat), is also known

as The Hidden Bird of Tāne[3] due to its association with the realms of the magical and nocturnal.

III   *The Evil Eye – the Touch – the Penalty*

The Laughing Owl, like the Morepork, gave a warning call of ill fortune.[4]

IV   *Away*

As its forest habitat was destroyed, and predators were introduced, the Laughing Owl, like many of New Zealand's unique endemic birds, disappeared.

V   *Herbs, Charms, and Wise Women*

For example, like the Kākā, the Laughing Owl was known to have been stung to death by introduced bees that were led by a famous queen.[5]

VI   *Astray, and Treasure*

The now extinct New Zealand Quail was known as *manu tohu* (Bird of Signs) because it was a portent of good fortune when fowlers heard it call out on their right-hand side, but of bad luck on their left.

VII   Banshees and Warnings

Young Tūī were tamed and taught to speak at isolated small
houses, secure from the distractions of noise and bustle.

IX   The Fighting of the Friends

Lessons were given near water, preferably beside a waterfall
where the splashing crystal-like droplets up above fought
with the dark swirling eddies deep below.

X   The Unquiet Dead

The accounts of the Patupaiarehe[6] share many similarities to
those folk-tales of the Irish fairies. This suggests fairy peo-
ples were once found all around the Earth in misty places.

XI   Appearances

If a fairy's voice could be heard keening, this was considered
a portent.

XII   Butter

The Sidhe were a fairy-people who favoured old Irish castles,
and like the Patupaiarehe, played a grand, sweet music using
wooden flutes.

XIII   The Fool of the Forth

The Irish peasant tells a tale of two classes of fairy, one like humans, and another that is wicked and full of spite.

XIV   Forths and Sheoguey[7] Places

The Māori too speak of two fairy classes: the fairy woodsmen and the maleficent Maero.

XV   Blacksmiths

Both Irish fairies and the Māori Patupaiarehe cannot bear fire, and the thundering death-coach of Ireland is mirrored by the *waka wairua* (the death omen of the ghost-canoe).

XVI   Monsters and Sheoguey Beasts

The hair of the dead was adorned with the wing feathers of the Albatross and the tail feathers of the vanished endemic Huia.

XVII   Friars and Priest Cures
       Two essays and notes by W. B. Yeats
       Witches and Wizards and Irish Folk-Lore
       Swedenborg, Mediums, and the Desolate Places

But despite these similarities to Ireland, the fairy lore of the Aotearoa forests has a distinct character that has evolved over centuries of living in harmony with Nature in a unique and glorious environment.

Afterword: Dawn Chorus Over the Sea

'This morn I was awakd by the singing of the birds ashore
from whence we are distant not a quarter of a mile, the num-
bers of them were certainly very great who seemd to strain
their throats with emulation perhaps; their voices were
certainly the most melodious wild musick I have ever heard,
almost imitating small bells but with the most tuneable silver
sound imaginable to which maybe the distance was no small
addition.'[8]

Postscript: Ringing in the Mountaintops

'Our linnet[9] is a little larger than the English, with a clear
bell-like voice, as of a blacksmith's hammer on an anvil.
Indeed, we might call him the harmonious blacksmith... Two
albatrosses came to my wool-shed about seven months ago,
and a dead one was found at Mount Peel not long since. I
did not see the former myself, but my cook, who was a sailor,
watched them for some time, and his word may be taken. I
believe, however, that their coming so far inland is a very
rare occurrence here.'[10]

Epilogue: A Lament

'It was a Māori "Lochaber No More," a lament for the
ancestral shieling from which the old stock — not unlike
the Highland crofters at the other end of the world — were
evicted by the new lords of the land with axe and fire-brand.
"Yet there are still fairies in the fastnesses of Ngongotaha,"
said Huhia. "On dim and cloudy days, and when the mists
descend and envelop the mountain side, the thin voices of

the *Patu-paiarehe* people may be heard, and also the sweet music of their flutes, the *putorino*, sounding very sweet, like spirit music, through the fog.'"[11]

The Grey Ghost: A Cathedral Organ, A Cathedral Tolling

Although the Kōkako's[12] treetop cathedral song is rarely heard, it carves into the minds of those favoured enough to hear it: "The cry of the crow is indescribably mournful. The wail of the wind through a leafless forest is cheerful compared to it. Perhaps the whistling of the wind through the neck of an empty whisky bottle is the nearest approach to it, and is sadly suggestive of departed spirits. Few people are aware that the crow is a song bird as it is only in the depths of the forest they can be heard to perfection. Their notes are very few but are the sweetest and most mellow toned I have ever heard a bird produce."[13]

Author's Notes:

1   Each of these entries under a roman numeral is copied from the *Contents* page
    of the 1970 edition of Lady Gregory's *Visions and Beliefs in the West of Ireland*,
    first published in 1920. Chapter VIII has been intentionally omitted.

2   Māori water-dwelling monster.

3   In Māori mythology, Tāne is the god of forests and birds.

4   Murdoch Riley, *Māori Bird Lore: An Introduction*, 2001.

5   H. Guthrie Smith, *Bird-life On a Run*, 1895.

6   Māori fairy-people.

7   The Anglicised term for Irish fairies. Sióg is the modern Irish word for a single
    fairy. The unreformed spelling is sídheóg, and Anglicised *sheogue*. (James
    MacKillop, *Dictionary of Celtic Mythology*, 2004.)

8   Joseph Banks, *The Endeavour Journal of Joseph Banks* 1768 – 1771, edited by
    J.C. Beaglehole, 1962.

9   The Bellbird or Makomako.

10 Samuel Butler, *A First Year in Canterbury Settlement*, 1863.

11 James Cowan, *Fairy Folk Tales of The Maori*, 1939.

12 Also known as the Grey Ghost or in this excerpt, as a crow.

13 Westland explorer Charlie Douglas' 1899 description of what he called the 'New
    Zealand crow' – the presumed extinct South Island Kōkako.

Priya Sarukkai Chabria
Manikkavachakar's Creation Hymns (Excerpts)

3.1-5

wobbling spheres round   into the elemental cosmos

                      immeasurable

            wonder beyond wonders

here our planet
         floats

impossible to sing these worlds' profuse beauties

try this for scale:
earth

    in its disk of stars

        a dust mote

           dancing

           among millions more

                in a shaft of light

that falls through a window of your home   the sunbeam Siva

3.124

solitary one

you
imbue immense earth with five qualities:
smell   taste   tactility   shape   rotations' sound Omkara

permeate water's four:
smell   taste   touch   sound

fire's three:
touch   sound   smell

air's elated two:
touch   sound

you are the expanding charge
of space

           rhapsodies   cinder   before reaching you

             life's oceans proliferate   because of you

          even gods in deepest dream   can't reach you

           yet this aimless cur — me —   you consecrate

                 lauds   lord   lauds   atomise

4.15-25

sperm-seed breaks
egg into life

the invisible throbs
vaguely visible

struggle
to survive uterine heat

eyes form
to remove darkness

organs pulse
their shapes

hear
the mother's heartbeat

filtered sounds
from the world beyond

struggle
to survive the womb's squeeze

struggle   push
break free from home

baby rests
in mother's bed

(each one's a seed almost invisible)

our bed's a roaring ocean of tears —
struggle

      for grace

           break free

2.37-42

ancient changelessness   who creates change

invisible towering one   seed of everything

outstripping wonder's stretch   yet encoding every atom

limitless

before

language arose   beyond

the silence of it uttermost ends   beyond

knowledge's reach   beyond

imagination   beyond

timelessness   but this too

yet snares himself in the bhakta's net

W.B. Yeats
The Phases of the Moon

An old man cocked his ear upon a bridge;
He and his friend, their faces to the South,
Had trod the uneven road. Their boots were soiled,
Their Connemara cloth worn out of shape;
They had kept a steady pace as though their beds,
Despite a dwindling and late-risen moon,
Were distant still. An old man cocked his ear.

AHERNE

What made that sound?

ROBARTES

                A rat or water-hen
Splashed, or an otter slid into the stream.
We are on the bridge; that shadow is the tower,
And the light proves that he is reading still.
He has found, after the manner of his kind,
Mere images; chosen this place to live in
Because, it may be, of the candle-light
From the far tower where Milton's Platonist
Sat late, or Shelley's visionary prince:
The lonely light that Samuel Palmer engraved,
An image of mysterious wisdom won by toil;
And now he seeks in book or manuscript
What he shall never find.

AHERNE

Why should not you
Who know it all ring at his door, and speak
Just truth enough to show that his whole life
Will scarcely find for him a broken crust
Of all those truths that are your daily bread;
And when you have spoken take the roads again?

ROBARTES

He wrote of me in that extravagant style
He had learned from Pater, and to round his tale
Said I was dead; and dead I choose to be.

AHERNE

Sing me the changes of the moon once more;
True song, though speech: 'mine author sung it me'.

ROBARTES

Twenty-and-eight the phases of the moon,
The full and the moon's dark and all the crescents,
Twenty-and-eight, and yet but six-and-twenty
The cradles that a man must needs be rocked in;
For there's no human life at the full or the dark.
From the first crescent to the half, the dream
But summons to adventure, and the man
Is always happy like a bird or a beast;
But while the moon is rounding towards the full
He follows whatever whim's most difficult
Among whims not impossible, and though scarred,
As with the cat-o'-nine-tails of the mind,

His body moulded from within his body
Grows comelier. Eleven pass, and then
Athena takes Achilles by the hair,
Hector is in the dust, Nietzsche is born,
Because the hero's crescent is the twelfth.
And yet, twice born, twice buried, grow he must,
Before the full moon, helpless as a worm.
The thirteenth moon but sets the soul at war
In its own being, and when that war's begun
There is no muscle in the arm; and after,
Under the frenzy of the fourteenth moon,
The soul begins to tremble into stillness,
To die into the labyrinth of itself!

    AHERNE

Sing out the song; sing to the end, and sing
The strange reward of all that discipline.

    ROBARTES

All thought becomes an image and the soul
Becomes a body: that body and that soul
Too perfect at the full to lie in a cradle,
Too lonely for the traffic of the world:
Body and soul cast out and cast away
Beyond the visible world.

    AHERNE

            All dreams of the soul
End in a beautiful man's or woman's body.

ROBARTES

Have you not always known it?

AHERNE

         The song will have it
That those that we have loved got their long fingers
From death, and wounds, or on Sinai's top,
Or from some bloody whip in their own hands.
They ran from cradle to cradle till at last
Their beauty dropped out of the loneliness
Of body and soul.

ROBARTES

The lover's heart knows that.

AHERNE

It must be that the terror in their eyes
Is memory or foreknowledge of the hour
When all is fed with light and heaven is bare.

ROBARTES

When the moon's full those creatures of the full
Are met on the waste hills by country men
Who shudder and hurry by: body and soul
Estranged amid the strangeness of themselves,
Caught up in contemplation, the mind's eye
Fixed upon images that once were thought,
For perfected, completed, and immovable

Images can break the solitude
Of lovely, satisfied, indifferent eyes.

And thereupon with aged, high-pitched voice
Aherne laughed, thinking of the man within,
His sleepless candle and laborious pen.

ROBARTES

And after that the crumbling of the moon:
The soul remembering its loneliness
Shudders in many cradles; all is changed.
It would be the world's servant, and as it serves,
Choosing whatever task's most difficult
Among tasks not impossible, it takes
Upon the body and upon the soul
The coarseness of the drudge.

AHERNE

                    Before the full
It sought itself and afterwards the world.

ROBARTES

Because you are forgotten, half out of life,
And never wrote a book, your thought is clear.
Reformer, merchant, statesman, learned man,
Dutiful husband, honest wife by turn,
Cradle upon cradle, and all in flight and all
Deformed, because there is no deformity
But saves us from a dream.

AHERNE

And what of those
That the last servile crescent has set free?

ROBARTES

Because all dark, like those that are all light,
They are cast beyond the verge, and in a cloud,
Crying to one another like the bats;
But having no desire they cannot tell
What's good or bad, or what it is to triumph
At the perfection of one's own obedience;
And yet they speak what's blown into the mind;
Deformed beyond deformity, unformed,
Insipid as the dough before it is baked,
They change their bodies at a word.

AHERNE

And then?

ROBARTES

When all the dough has been so kneaded up
That it can take what form cook Nature fancies,
The first thin crescent is wheeled round once more.

AHERNE

But the escape; the song's not finished yet.

ROBARTES

Hunchback and Saint and Fool are the last crescents.
The burning bow that once could shoot an arrow
Out of the up and down, the wagon-wheel
Of beauty's cruelty and wisdom's chatter —
Out of that raving tide — is drawn betwixt
Deformity of body and of mind.

AHERNE

Were not our beds far off I'd ring the bell,
Stand under the rough roof-timbers of the hall
Beside the castle door, where all is stark
Austerity, a place set out for wisdom
That he will never find; I'd play a part;
He would never know me after all these years
But take me for some drunken country man;
I'd stand and mutter there until he caught
'Hunchback and Saint and Fool', and that they came
Under the three last crescents of the moon,
And then I'd stagger out. He'd crack his wits
Day after day, yet never find the meaning.

And then he laughed to think that what seemed hard
Should be so simple – a bat rose from the hazels
And circled round him with its squeaky cry,
The light in the tower window was put out.

From Klamath Folklore
Incantation Songs

Song of the fire-mantle:
 Lû'luksash nû shkutíya
 In fire-flames I am enveloped

The incantation sings:
 Shuî'sh hátak nû géna nû
 I the song I am walking here

Song of the blind girl:
 Lúashtka nû lû'tchipka
 käíla nákant nî lúyapka
 In the fog I am straying blind
 All over the earth I am wandering

Song of the skō'ks or spirits:
 Ḳakó pîla nû la-uláwa
 Reduced to mere bones, I rattle through the air

Conjurer's own song:

Käílanti nû shî'lshîla

I, the earth, am resounding like the roll of thunder

Song of the gray fox:

Nánuktua nû papî'sh gî

Everything I can devour

Song of the eagle-feather:

Mû'kash a gî nû, gená nû, hō

I am the eagle-feather, I am going down, hō

Unknown song:

Sháppashti nû lakí gî

I am the lord of the sun

Editors' Note:

These particular incantations, with the exception of the last two, specifically come from the 'Klamath Lake People'.

Autumn Richardson
Incipience

Sit calmly, spine anchored into earth. *Generatrix*. Stones
vibrate with their potencies. Radiate what they have gathered
from astronomical bodies.

Watch the grey ocean. Its abrading fingers, its undulating
skins erode the certainty of earth. Solidity collapses and
viscera spills to waves.

~

Seeds pour forth in limitless patterns. Birds are the shapes of
their secret knowledge. Hoof-prints in snow, the admixing of
clouds, the mycelial threadings of rivers — each are signals;
pharos flickering. Sigils welling up through mud and bone.

~

A plant stem encloses new tissue over its wound — a callous teeming with regenerative cells. We too can do this, self-suture our injuries. Alter our chemistry.

A gall can be a thing of beauty, a scar increase harmony. Toxins can become tinctures in the blood; remedies against future malady.

~

Polysensual earth, a hoard of light beneath its skin, pulsing saps within its stalks.

Incipience, is always, and ever, the law.

haŋ-ye'-tu-wi

the night-sun, the moon

ta-sa'-pa

the black bear in the sacred dialect

wa-kaŋ'

a spirit, something consecrated

wi'-ḣmuŋ-ġe

witch-medicine

Charlotte Mary Mew
The Forest Road

The forest road,
The infinite straight road stretching away
World without end: the breathless road between the walls
Of the black listening trees: the hushed, grey road
Beyond the window that you shut to-night
Crying that you would look at it by day —
There is a shadow there that sings and calls
But not for you. Oh! hidden eyes that plead in sleep
Against the lonely dark, if I could touch the fear
And leave it kissed away on quiet lids —
If I could hush these hands that are half-awake,
Groping for me in sleep I could go free.
I wish that God would take them out of mine
And fold them like the wings of frightened birds
Shot cruelly down, but fluttering into quietness so soon,
Broken, forgotten things; there is no grief for them in the
        green Spring
When the new birds fly back to the old trees.
But it shall not be so with you. I will look back. I wish I
        knew that God would stand
Smiling and looking down on you when morning comes,
To hold you, when you wake, closer than I,
So gently though: and not with famished lips or hungry arms:
He does not hurt the frailest, dearest things
As we do in the dark. See, dear, your hair —
I must unloose this hair that sleeps and dreams
About my face, and clings like the brown weed
To drowned, delivered things, tossed by the tired sea
Back to the beaches. Oh! your hair! If you had lain

A long time dead on the rough, glistening ledge
Of some black cliff, forgotten by the tide,
The raving winds would tear, the dripping brine would rust
away
Fold after fold of all the loveliness
That wraps you round, and makes you, lying here,
The passionate fragrance that the roses are.
But death would spare the glory of your head
In the long sweetness of the hair that does not die:
The spray would leap to it in every storm,
The scent of the unsilenced sea would linger on
In these dark waves, and round the silence that was you —
Only the nesting gulls would hear — but there would still be
whispers in your hair;
Keep them for me; keep them for me. What *is* this singing
on the road
That makes all other music like the music in a dream —
Dumb to the dancing and the marching feet; you know, in
dreams, you see
Old pipers playing that you cannot hear,
And ghostly drums that only seem to beat. This seems to
climb:
Is it the music of a larger place? It makes our room too small:
it is like a stair,
A calling stair that climbs up to a smile you scarcely see,
Dim, but so waited for; and *you* know what a smile is, how it
calls,
How if I smiled you always ran to me.
Now you must sleep forgetfully, as children do.

There is a Spirit sits by us in sleep
Nearer than those who walk with us in the bright day.
I think he has a tranquil, saving face: I think he came
Straight from the hills: he may have suffered there in time
    gone by,
And once, from those forsaken heights, looked down,
Lonely himself, on all the lonely sorrows of the earth.
It is his kingdom — Sleep. If I could leave you there —
If, without waking you, I could get up and reach the door —!
We used to go together. — Shut, scared eyes,
Poor, desolate, desperate hands, it is not I
Who thrust you off. No, take your hands away —
I cannot strike your lonely hands. Yes, I have struck your
    heart,
It did not come so near. Then lie you there
Dear and wild heart behind this quivering snow
With two red stains on it: and I will strike and tear
Mine out, and scatter it to yours. Oh! throbbing dust,
You that were life, our little wind-blown hearts!
             The road! the road!
There is a shadow there: I see my soul,
I hear my soul, singing among the trees!

Jane Lovell
nunatak:

a stone ridge exposed by wind,
a lip of stone curled at the glaucous wind,
its harrying across blown snow;

a skyline ridge, blade-and-socket spine
of something fossilised, claws sunk
in the hidden world below;

a ridge of stone, a pebbled egg
abandoned in its cleft, the embryo
a shock of livid skin in frozen oils;

a granite ridge, its icebound edge
orbited by tracks of lupine shadow
swerving out across the void.

Marcus Aurelius Antoninus
The Meditations (Excerpts)

You exist as part of a whole. You will disappear again in
that which produced you; or rather you will change and be
resumed again into the productive intelligence.

*

Many grains of frankincense are laid on the same altar. One
falls soon, another later. It makes no difference.

*

Order not your life as though you had ten thousand years to live. Fate hangs over you. While you live, while yet you may, be good.

*

I am in tune with all that is of thy harmony, O Nature. For me nothing is too early and nothing is too late that comes in thy good time. All is fruit to me, O Nature, that thy seasons bring. From thee are all things, thou comprehendest all, and all returns to thee.

*

Observe continually that all things exist in change; and keep this thought ever with you, that Nature loves nothing more than changing what things now are, and making others like them. For what now is, is in a manner the seed of what shall be.

*

Ever consider this Universe as one living being, with one material substance and one spirit. Observe how all things are referred to the one intelligence of this being; how all things act on one impulse; how all things are concurrent causes of all others; and how all things are connected and intertwined.

*

Time is a river, a violent torrent of things coming into being. Each one, as soon as it has appeared, is swept away: it is succeeded by another which is swept away in its turn.

*

Everything material is soon engulfed in the matter of the whole, and every active cause is swiftly resumed into the Universal reason. The memory of all things is quickly buried in eternity.

*

Do you dread change? What can come without it? What can be pleasanter or more proper to universal nature? Can you heat your bath unless wood undergoes a change? Can you be fed unless a change is wrought upon your food? Can any useful thing be done without changes? Do you not see, then, that this change also which is working in you is even such as these, and alike necessary to the nature of the Universe?

*

Presiding nature from the universal substance, as from wax, now forms a horse, now breaks it up again, making of its matter a tree, afterwards a man, and again something different. Each of these shapes subsists but for a little.

*

In a little space Nature, the supreme and universal ruler, will change all things that you behold; out of their substance she will make other things, and others again out of the substance of these, so that the Universe may be ever new.

*

This from Plato: 'To the man who has true grandeur of mind, and who contemplates all time and all being, can human life appear a great matter? "Impossible", says the other. "Can then such a one count death a thing of dread?" "'No, indeed.'"

*

Look inward. Within is the fountain of Good. Dig constantly and it will ever well forth.

*

The horse, the vine — all things are formed for some purpose. Where is the wonder? Even the sun saith, 'I was formed for a certain work'; and similarly the other Gods. For what end are you formed?

Aashish Kaul
Blue in Green

No one now remembers A.S. Kalan. And yet, to have discovered him one winter morning in a basement store made life and art intersect in a way that frightened me, shattered the year-old gloom, and nudged me on a journey that still continues to unravel.

The day was cold. A fumy end-of-year mist clawed the peeling, grime-encrusted walls, softened the sounds, and soothed the sun into a lunar disc. The heart clings to such insignificant details: under the hungry stare of a kestrel perched on a rusted tin roof, the left turn into the busy narrow lane off the market square, passing the light smoke rising from the small coal pot blunting and warming the mound before the peanut vendor, sidestepping the magazine stand and then, directly opposite the fruit kiosk and partly concealed by the shoeshine stationed as if to block the way, taking the age-smoothened staircase to the level below.

It was only slightly darker between the overfull shelves.

The book must have been there a long time, an unread copy
ageing from neglect and the stale air of the establishment,
its script darkening over the slow-spreading yellow spots
through the pages. But the glossy black cover, the soft blue
and yellow strokes of Emil Nolde's *Lake Lucerne* adorning
the front, and the undamaged spine gave no indication of
age. Hidden and unclaimed, it lay behind the recent sen-
sations of the season. What prevailing indulgent spirit had
brushed my elbow, upsetting the pile on the shelf's edge, to
make me look deeper?

On the spine was the totemic wild cat colophon, spotted,
bewhiskered and radiant in white, balanced on one paw with
its tail and limbs fanning out like a dancing Indian divinity,
then the author's name in italics, followed by the title in
capitals: 'CONVERSATIONS IN COMO'.

Removing it then from the bottom of the shelf, I had
almost expected to find a swift voice weaving the tempo of
scenes, the oblique tact of entering and recording landscape,
settings dreamily distant but not far, poetic moments glisten-
ing like dew drops on the leafskin of the text. It looked that
kind of book.

There were those things, but beneath them and obvious
from the beginning, making them secondary or rather nat-
ural, was something intangible spreading through the text,
conjoining theme, form, and intent in a river rush of act and
meaning which gave the impression not of observing a piece
of life but properly entering it. Like thorny gales unburden-
ing a tree of its lushness, the prose had been pared down
in cool discernment, lending to its mood the hue of myth.
Every book, said Borges, begins as a mirror of the world and
ends up being another thing added to the world's contents.
Yet here in my hands was a rarity not merely contesting this
duality but surpassing it through synthesis.

How had he done it, this overspill of life into text?

Reading, that noble art, nobler than writing, resists the innocence without which no writer can begin. Kalan, it seemed, was aware of this conflict, had taken his time to fully absorb its lesson. He had come to his task the least innocent of writers, without vanity, that twin of innocence, ceding the wish for authority and distance as if he had no purchase on such things, writing from a state of fragility as he watched his memories drop into words and turn to fiction, and so succeeded where others surer of their vocation may have struggled. It was a sobering reminder of an old lesson: to keep innocent enthusiasm at bay, to be rather like the wise reader in her moments of absorption, captivated yet clinical.

In some ways it was a simple book, telling the story of its protagonist from his years of boyhood and youth up until middle age, the hopes and disappointments, love and its travails, gossamer emotions tearing apart on the rock of reality. Up to a point it behaved like a *Bildungsroman*, then wavered and dissolved in a crosscurrent of themes.

How hopeless it feels now to give a sense of its style or qualities, the hopelessness itself the measure of its superiority. Because Kalan employed the essayistic register in telling his story, he could paint its settings and characters in broad strokes, leaving out all extraneous material and going straight for the thing in its facticity, moving with a swiftness reminiscent of Pushkin, that lover of classical balance, and producing all at once authority, atmosphere, and distance: facts so purified and distilled as to appear fictitious.

As the day grew bolder, as the sun clutched the earth through the tattered banner of clouds, as the west wind gathered, as the din sharpened in the emptying sky, as the day waned and forms gently vibrated along the fringes, as darkness dissolved drop by weightless drop in the chilling air, as dim stars struggled for purchase on the city's sodium sky, I allowed myself to be led by that calm voice through a steepening descent into the book's fluid depths.

In the region of Lombardy, above the rich shores of Lake Como, in a seventeenth-century villa, more Bhutanese than Italianate in profile, thrilling amidst its copses and gardens covering the promontory that forked the lake, near which Manzoni and Stendhal had once lived, the unnamed protagonist sat conversing with the writer John Hawkes and a woman named Clara.

Kalan did not relate what was exchanged between them in this instance, except alluding to past conversations that lent the book its suggestively simple title, ending instead with a sustained meditation on his near obsession with the spectral quality of remote mountain lakes he had travelled to at different times in his life. The book's final image was of his silent listeners: Hawkes already in shadow as the sunset, melting on Clara's cheek, shook the lake free of its blue silk, lifting it into the evening mist over the surrounding woods and glades and softening the glitter of ice in the faraway crags under the first stars. The night, so went the concluding line, waited beyond the dusk song of the owls.

The book ended, but the mood remained. Then the book began to recede and the mood seemed to lighten.

But it was deceptive, this lessening. The story grew even as it faded, gathered strength, turned in the distance, drenched me in its spindrift. Gradually, it began to unsettle me. In the course of a few weeks, I could no longer ignore the questions. What was Hawkes thinking in those twilight moments? Who was Clara? And, most importantly (but why?), where was Kalan?

*

Faint enquiring cries easily vanishing into the day's cruel coarseness. Faint but not insubstantial.

Details about the author were few, if crucial. Kalan was born in 1942 in pre-independence India. He had studied toward degrees in geology in India and literature in the United States. He had held appointments at Buffalo, Johns Hopkins, and then for some years at Brown, where he must have met Hawkes. He had written at least two other books: *Clara*, a second work of prose fiction, and *The Lover's Mask*, a study of Stendhal's heroines (no further publication details were offered).

Weeks of searching uncovered nothing aside from a brief review in an old London supplement. Then Gina — down each day in the public library partly for her own research and partly from a wish to escape the distress of a relationship gone sour and that, oddly, made her pore over the book I had lent her — dug up two interviews of Kalan, one given to a student journal at Brown, and another in the literary magazine *Stand*.

In the first, more reportage than interview, Kalan came across as mostly reticent, deflecting questions about his own writing with a refined randomness. Even then a stray remark or two was revealing: the rift between language and landscape that for him was forever unbridgeable, his nostalgia for older literatures, their ease of design or voice that could now not be emulated. The struggle to lay bare this nostalgia through the synergies of dream, desire, and death was all to which he had ever aspired.

So the swiftness of register I had assumed as somehow belonging to that polished and closed continental sensibility — the crucible in which the art of the novel was properly forged in nineteenth-century Europe — was only half the story. The writing achieved its full effect from the deftness with which it masked its colonial roots. This was no easy task, and it did more than add to Kalan's success — it showed his ability to put form in service of his own historical location, to use language like music, to use silence as weft, to say things one felt couldn't be said in a language foreign to the landscape. There lay the reason of its appeal to me.

On being asked, at another point, what he was presently reading, he had replied: Jan Zwicky's *Wittgenstein Elegies*, and, in a burst of openness, had called it the best thing he had read in the entire year.

Then there was the grainy black and white picture of the author, the only one I ever saw, which made him real and not a hoax. A lean square face, cheeks pinched near the slightly flaring nostrils, eyes, dark, shining, full of great depth, that made the face look as if it was just now emerging from the surrounding darkness. Hair still quite full, making him look at once younger and older than his years.

The latter, longer, interview was conducted while Kalan was in Britain, just upon his return from a month-long hiking trip in the Scottish Highlands. He had gone up the steep basalt slope of the main ridge to see the mist-drenched Cuillin massif in the Isle of Skye, he had perambulated, as if in a religious fervour, Loch Lomond and Loch Tay, he had stayed at Ardmay on the shores of Loch Long, catching now and then the snaky drone of a bagpipe dying above the darkening lake, and had later visited the Cairngorms in homage to the local naturalist and poet Nan Shepherd. He had travelled south to the town of Keswick and the village of Grasmere in the Lake District, paying the obligatory visit to Dove cottage, nestled amidst the peculiar quiet — an effect of the shifting light beams cutting through the clouds — of the Cumbrian fells, finally arriving in Suffolk at the invitation of the poet and translator Michael Hamburger.

Languid talk about poetry, landscape, and mortality. Investigations into the nature of words, geology, the birth of matter. So much so that at times it was difficult to tell apart the interviewee from the interviewer: Kalan easily rising into those sublime realms he had only recently left behind, realms such as, he professed, he had encountered in Hamburger's own work, while the poet time and again pulling him down to the texts themselves, asking this or that question about his books or motivations, which he always answered tangentially, raising other questions in turn, pointing to other writers, other moments of other writers. Trakl, Broch, Vallejo, Izumi Shikibu — names thrown up by the exaltation, or simply the exhaustion, of literature, by the gathering shadows of the past and the evening.

The mood entered me, and in a few paragraphs I found that opening between text and world where scenes behind the rush of contextual thought are laid bare — wind caught and made matter in the spreading yew tree by the fence, the low-angled, slow majestic rise of the geese over the marsh, cattle lowering their eyes in repose under a bird's jangling whistle, the taste of light, half-cold tea — until suddenly I came across the reference to a pair of gloves in Kalan's second work, *Clara*, which Hamburger felt was charged with a revelatory energy, a function not of the clarity or the particular stance of language but of the tear they opened in the fullness of the world.

He recalled the time. It had been in Berlin, the city of Hamburger's childhood, in the months following the collapse of the Wall, a strange but creatively fulfilling period of his life. What he now remembered most, however, were the banal details, like those car dealerships that had materialised almost overnight on the other side.

At the end came the customary question about current or future projects. Nothing, he said, except that I am going home.

So he had returned to India — and if fiction was thought

to reveal the whole truth — to his family home in the hills. This would have been two decades ago, and in two full decades he hadn't published a single new work or appeared at a public event or gathering. He seemed entirely unconcerned about the fate of his books. In a world bursting with books, perhaps this was the only sane response. Or perhaps he had passed away in the meantime.

I left the piece on the desk and, turning away the lamp, closed my eyes. The room had grown cold, but from the other side came the warmth of Davis's horn.

C.S. Mills
In a rare east wind

After the equinox a rare east wind blows across the moraine,
tumbling backward over dunes and bent pine. Water beads
up along waxy blades, and the chorus speaks, twelve as one:

> *Call it pliant stem, rising precipitate, thin song,*
> *call it wind-rose, forked branch,*
> *call it gesture*

Jack pine needles divide the wind into countless streams,
and it converges again in the lee. A sharp-keeled stone
splits the wind in two for a continuous instant. The chorus
continues:

> *Call it Proteus, arc of spiral, all-centre,*
> *call it phasing moon-disc, both-in-each,*
> *call it iridescence*

The east wind tumbles over the brink and carries out over
dark water toward sky. The chorus concludes, equivocally:

> *It is settling air, deep lens, dispassionate gaze,*
> *and while it has no name we know,*
> *it may answer to silence*

Christine Morro
kinship

walking in a crepuscular shadow map
naked foot slips into a narrow wedge of light

here above the empty field a bird rises
in a flickering helix, heart as cave as altar

a slender luminous crescent, receptive and clear
looks down like the eye of a god

in the darkness beyond
rests a body of stars, each pulse of light recorded
before you were born

a fragile alliance of seed heads glows at dawn
aroused from lassitude by a sharpening love we call sun

we have no navigational codes for courage

each act of witness becomes a sacred ritual

~

i draw a circle of fire to warm and to seed
that which has not yet been shaped in dreams
before thumb presses into clay, fire is
the body, formless, fire is air

breath precedes flesh
inspiration. voice. vishuddha.
in the vastness where earth meets sea
sky and fire kindle life

receptive, i am vessel clear and pure
i am invitation, prana
life-giving force

i draw a circle of fire
within the circle an inverse triangle
listening is alchemical

tied to mystery i call into being
that which has not yet eyes

flickering embers become a skein
of geese, a carbon smudge tapering
above horizon

i carry the fire

~

yield to the things we cannot name
the source of belonging
wildness

sacred mantras
silent words offerings
passing over, under over, under
integrated loam. heath.

kinship

crown and sacrum
to remember is to honour

made of earth, water, wind
a circle etched by the solitary blade
of coarse sea grass

o′-ha

a straight place in a river

ta′-ḣiŋ-ća-ha

a deer skin

o-o′-o-ka-ṡtaŋ

the Balsam of Life

taku wakaŋ

the Great Spirit

End Matter
Notes & Bibliography

New Work

Peter Mark Adams
    Star Axis, New Mexico / Reflections
Dan Beachy-Quick
    Canto VII
Priya Sarukkai Chabria
    Manikkavachakar's Creation Hymns (Excerpts)
Roz Quillan Chandler
    the past is
Jake Crist
    Protean Étude
Kim Dorman
    Kerala Journal (Excerpts)
Jasmine Gallagher
    In Loving Memory Of
James Goodman
    Ends of saints
Brian Johnstone
    A Lock of Fleece
Aashish Kaul
    Blue in Green
Steffi Lang
    At Slaty Fork
    Residual
Jane Lovell
    Landmarks
    nunatak:

Jay Merill
> *The Four Winds*

C.S. Mills
> *Apian heathen hof*
> *A visitor at the end of winter*
> *In a rare east wind*

Christine Morro
> *haunt*
> *kinship*

Paul Prudence
> *Scholar's Rocks*

Autumn Richardson
> *Incipience*

Penelope Shuttle
> *Retrieved Data (Excerpts)*

Richard Skelton
> *The Body from Scaleby Moss*

Judi Sutherland
> *Following Teisa (Excerpt)*

Archive Sources

W.H.I. Bleek and L.C. Lloyd
> *Specimens of Bushman Folklore*, 1911

Thomas Browne
> *The Religio Medici and Other Writings*, 1937

Franz Boas
> *Tsimshian Myths*, 1916

George W. Chrystal
> *The Meditations of the Emperor Marcus Aurelius Antoninus*, 1902

Albert Samuel Gatschet
> *The Klamath Indians of Southwestern Oregon*, 1890

Lady Gregory
  Gods and Fighting Men, 1904
John Gower
  Confessio Amantis, 1889
Robert Hooke
  Micrographia, 1665
Magda Isanos
  Poems, 1943
Walter K. Kelly
  Curiosities of Indo-European Tradition and Folklore, 1863
R.P. Masani
  Folklore of Wells, 1918
Charlotte Mary Mew
  Saturday Market, 1921
Elias Steinmeyer and Eduard Sievers
  Die Althochdeutschen Glossen, 1895
Edward Step
  Wayside and Woodland Trees, 1940
Janil Uc Tun
  Colección de insectos que volaron sobre mi cabeza, 2020
W.B. Yeats
  A Vision, 1937

Word Lists

Words from *Grammar and Dictionary of the Dakota Language* by S.R. Riggs, 1851. The Dakota are an indigenous people of North America. Their original territory, according to Rigg, extended 'from the Mississippi river on the east to the Black Hills on the west, and from the mouth of the Big Sioux river on the south to Devil's Lake on the north'.

Permissions

Janil Uc Tun's *Colección de insectos que volaron sobre mi cabeza* was first published by The Ofi Press in 2020. It is reproduced in part here with the kind permission of Jack Little and ProHispan.

Notes

Wherever possible, original spelling and punctuation have been preserved in the archive texts.

With Thanks

The editors would like to extend their thanks to the contributors, without whom *Reliquiae* would not be possible. They would also like to express heartfelt thanks to each *Friend* and *Patron* of Corbel Stone Press, whose continued support is most gratefully received.

Lightning Source UK Ltd.
Milton Keynes UK
UKHW010409291020
372426UK00001B/18